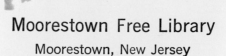

EDWARD II

Edward II – the Gloucester effigy

EDWARD II

Harold F. Hutchison

I must have wanton poets, pleasant wits,
Musicians, that with touching of a string
May draw the pliant king which way I please.

Marlowe, *Edward the Second*,
Act 1, scene i, 51–3

STEIN AND DAY/*Publishers*/New York

T O
HELEN, ANNABEL
AND TOBY

First published in the United States of America
by Stein and Day/*Publishers* 1972
Copyright © 1971 Harold F. Hutchison
Library of Congress Catalog Card No. 71-184654
Printed in the United States of America
Stein and Day/*Publishers*/7 East 48 Street, New York, N.Y. 10017
ISBN 0-8128-1448-7

CONTENTS

ILLUSTRATIONS

MAPS

Drawn by W. Bromage

SOURCES
AND
ABBREVIATIONS

Invaluable bibliographies are to be found in Professor May McKisack's *The Fourteenth Century* (Oxford 1959), 533–66, and in the late Professor Hilda Johnstone's appendix to her chapter XIV of *The Cambridge Medieval History*, VII, 881–7.

The following abbreviations are used in the Notes:

A.H.R.	*American Historical Review.*
Ann. Lond.	*Annales Londonienses* in *Stubbs Chronicles* (q.v.) I, 3–251.
Ann. Paul.	*Annales Paulini* in as above, I, 255–370.
Baker	*Chronica Galfridi le Baker de Swynebroke*, ed. E. Maunde Thompson (Oxford, 1889).
Barbour Bruce	J. Barbour, *The Bruce*, ed. W. M. Mackenzie (London, 1909).
Bower	*Johannis de Fordun Scotichronicon cum Supplementis et Continuatione Walteri Bower*, ed. W. Goodall (Edinburgh, 1759).
Bridlington	*Gesta Edwardi de Caernarvon auctore canonico Bridlingtoniensi* in *Stubbs Chronicles* (q.v.) II, 25–151.
Brut	*The Brut or The Chronicles of England*, ed. F. W. D. Brie (Oxford, 1906), I, 187–253.
C.D.S.	*Calendar of Documents relating to Scotland*, ed. Baih (Edinburgh, 1881–8).
Chapters	T. F. Tout, *Chapters in Medieval Administrative History* (Manchester, 1937), II.
Chron. Ford.	*J. de Fordun Cronica Gentis Scotorum*, ed. W. F. Skene (Edinburgh, 1871–2).

Chron. Lond.	*The Chronicles of London,* ed. and trans. E. Goldsmid (Edinburgh, 1885), II, 5–48.
C.M.H.	H. Johnstone in *Cambridge Mediaeval History* (Cambridge, 1932), VII chap. XIV, 412–32 and 881–7.
D.N.B.	*Dictionary of National Biography.*
E.H.R.	*English Historical Review.*
Flores Hist.	*Flores Historiarum,* ed. H. G. Luard (Rolls Series, 1890).
Genesis	J. H. Ramsay, *Genesis of Lancaster* (Oxford, 1913), I, 1–182.
Guisborough	*The Chronicles of Walter of Guisborough previously edited as the Chronicle of Walter Hemingford or Hemingburgh,* ed. H. Rothwell for the Royal Historical Society (London, 1957).
Higden	*Polychronicon Ranulphi Higden monachi Cestrensis* with *the English translations of John Trevisa* etc. ed. J. R. Lumby (Rolls Series, 1965), VIII.
Knighton	*Chronicon Henrici Knighton,* ed. J. R. Lumby, (Rolls Series, 1895), I
Lanercost	*Chronicon de Lanercost,* trans. H. Maxwell (Glasgow, 1913).
Langtoft	*Chronicle of Pierre de Langtoft,* ed. T. Wright (Rolls Series, 1867).
Letters	*Letters of Edward Prince of Wales 1304–5,* ed. H. Johnstone (Roxburghe Club, 1951).
Maddicott	J. R. Maddicott, *Thomas of Lancaster 1307–1322* (Oxford, 1970).
Melsa	*Chronica monasterii de Melsa* (Meaux), ed. W. D. Macray (Rolls Series, 1863).
Murimuth	*Adae Murimuth Continuatio Chronicorum,* ed. E. M. Thompson (Rolls Series, 1889).
Place	T. F. Tout, *The Place of the reign of Edward II in English History,* 2nd ed. revised by H. Johnstone (Manchester, 1936).
Rishanger	*Willelmi Rishanger Chronica et Annales in Chronica Monasterii S. Albani,* ed. H. T. Riley (Rolls Series, 1865).

Rot. Parl.	*Rotuli Parliamentorum* (Records Commission, 1777).
Rymer	*Foedera Conventiones Litterae et cujuscumque Acta Publica inter Reges Anglos et alios,* ed. T. Rymer (Records Commission, 1816–69).
Scalacronica	*Scalacronica* by Sir Thomas Gray of Heton, Kt. ed. J. Stevenson (Maitland Club, 1836).
Scotichronicon	See *Bower* above.
S.H.R.	*Scottish Historical Review.*
Stat.	*Statutes of the Realm* (Records Commission, 1810–22).
Stubbs Chronicles	W. Stubbs, *Chronicles of the Reigns of Edward I and Edward II* (Rolls Series, 1965), I and II.
Trevet	*F. Nicholai Triveti Annales,* ed. T. Hogg for English Historical Society, 1845.
Trevisa	See *Higden* above.
T.R.H.S.	*Transactions of the Royal Historical Society.*
Trokelowe	*Johannes de Trokelowe etc. Chronica et Annales,* ed. H. T. Riley (Rolls Series, 1866).
Vita	*Vita Edwardi Secundi Monachi Cuiusdam Malmesberiensis,* ed. and trans. N. Denholm-Young (London, 1957).
Walsingham	*Historia Anglicana Thomas Walsingham,* ed. H. T. Riley (Rolls Series, 1863), I.

FOREWORD

So far as I know there is no complete biography of Edward of
Caernarvon. There is however an interesting volume in the
British Museum entitled *The History of the Life, Reign and Death of
Edward II, King of England and Lord of Ireland, with the Rise and
Fall of his great Favourites, Gaveston and the Spencers*, written by
'E. F.'[1] in the year 1627 and published in London in 1680. It is
beautifully written but full of historical inaccuracies, and of
course it only deals with Edward's reign – it does not adequately
cover even his death. The author is supposed to have been
the cultured and witty Henry Cary, Viscount Falkland (d.
1633).

On the other hand, Edward's death has given posterity a
great Marlowe tragedy. Marlowe, I think, understood Edward
of Caernarvon much better than most subsequent historians
and researchers. He was more alive to the poetry and tragedy of
homosexuality, and he was lucky to have lived in an age which
was less hypocritical and less shamefaced about all sensuality
than any other age save our own. His Edward 'frolics with his
minion', his plot is woven round revenge for the minion's
murder, and the climax of the play is a rapid sequence of
deposition, foul murder and immediate nemesis which is
history justifiably telescoped in the interests of magnificent
drama. In less heroic vein Edward's quarrels with his barons
have given distinguished constitutional historians ample scope
for much expert if disputatious research, and the exceptionally
full records of administration during the reign have provided
Professor T. F. Tout, one of our greatest historians, and his
school with generous materials for fascinating and learned
analysis of its detailed working. Edward's youth and his death

[1] A poor version of E.F.'s History was edited by the antiquary William
Oldys (a friend of Dr Johnson) with additional notes by Thomas Park in
Vol. I of the *Harleian Miscellany* (London, 1808), 67–95.
For E.F.'s conclusion see note 4, p. 153 below.

I

have been the subject of specialist monographs, the importance of his reign has been contrasted with the alleged incompetence of the man in a famous larger work by Tout, the baronial opposition to him has warranted a brilliantly exhaustive study by Dr J. Conway Davies, and his letters during a vital period of his early manhood have been perfectly edited by the late Professor Hilda Johnstone. There is also a wide range of medieval chronicles and official records extant (and since printed) of which some are contemporary. There is, therefore, no lack of sources, both primary and secondary, and I have consulted them all.

In general histories of recent date, Edward II has usually been dismissed as a despicable failure who reaped the just reward of his incompetence and, by inference, of his immorality, and whose chief claim to mention has been that he lost the battle of Bannockburn. In the chronicles there is usually nothing but ill-concealed contempt. Such unqualified vituperation, however, tends to stimulate a certain sympathy for a victim who cannot defend himself. I plead guilty to such an unscientific reaction in myself, but in studying all the sources I have found some evidence for confirming that reaction. It is true, as Hilda Johnstone shrewdly commented in the *Cambridge Medieval History*, that modern research 'has not so far altered traditional values as to make Edward I a small man or Edward II a great one'. But it is also true, as May McKisack writes in *The Fourteenth Century*, that 'we may pity the weak-willed prince, successor to a famous father, to whom fell not only the administrative problems endemic in the medieval state but also the *damnosa hereditas* of a hostile Scotland, financial chaos and an over-mighty cousin'. I have come to couple my pity with the conclusion that Edward of Caernarvon was not the nonentity most historians would have us believe.

I have therefore tried to present a valid portrait of the reign from Edward's point of view – a portrait of Edward as a human being as well as a king – and I have therefore eschewed the minutiae of administrative and constitutional research, which can be found adequately elucidated elsewhere. I have not tried to whitewash a scoundrel, to make a saint out of a sinner, or to elevate a rather odd personality into a prodigy of genius, but I have tried to present a sympathetic portrait in the round rather than a black and white caricature.

This book could not have been written without the help of the works of the late Professor T. F. Tout, of Professor May McKisack, of the late Professor Hilda Johnstone and of Dr J. Conway Davies – to all of them I owe my grateful thanks, while of course absolving them from any responsibility for my own interpretations and conclusions. It is only to be regretted that none of them have summed up their scholarship in a full-scale complete history of the reign. Until that major work is available I offer this book as a humble contribution to a debate that will continue whenever students of our past ponder the tragic fates of Peter of Gaveston, of Thomas of Lancaster, of both the Despensers and of Edward of Caernarvon.

Finally, I wish to register my most grateful thanks for the kindness and helpfulness of the staff of the British Museum, and for the encouragement and patience of my wife, who has always so efficiently typed my untidy and illspelt manuscripts.

HAROLD F. HUTCHISON

Hove, Sussex. 1971

Chapter 1

EDWARD
OF
CAERNARVON

King Edward I was a man of giant physique, abnormally long
life and overpowering energy – and he was married twice. It is
therefore not surprising that his family was large – in all he had
six sons and ten daughters. In the spring of 1284 his first queen,
Eleanor of Castile, was with him in Wales where he was com-
pleting arrangements for superimposing English supremacy
upon Welsh intransigence, and so, he hoped, settling his Welsh
difficulties once and for all. While the king was busy at Rhuddlan, his pregnant queen was housed in temporary special
quarters at Caernarvon, where a great new castle and walled
town were being built to supersede the original 'motte and
bailey' of the Normans. There, on 25 April – the unpropitious
St Mark's Day – Queen Eleanor gave birth to her fourth son,
who was consequently to be known as Edward of Caernarvon.
Her first two sons had died in infancy, but the third, Alfonso, a
boy of eleven, was already recognized as heir to the throne.[1]

The famous story of how Edward of Caernarvon was cere-
monially presented to the native Welsh leaders in witty fulfil-
ment of his father's pledge that he would provide them with a
prince 'that was borne in Wales and could speake never a word
of English', was first recorded in Elizabethan times, and it
acquired some authority from its inclusion in the *Annales* of
John Stow. But its provenance is more than doubtful – Alfonso

[1] *Flores Hist.*, III, 61 and n. Alfonso had acted as his father's deputy in
presenting to Westminster Abbey the spoils of his father's victory over
Prince Llywelyn ap Gruffydd.

5

was the acknowledged heir to the throne, and it is unlikely that a younger son would have received endowment before provision had been made for the elder. Even in recent times, a small room in the magnificent Eagle Tower of Caernarvon Castle has been described as the site of this ceremony, but, when Queen Eleanor was in Caernarvon, the building of the Eagle Tower had only just begun. Sadly, the charming story must remain only a legend.[1]

In August 1284 Alfonso suddenly died, and Edward of Caernarvon took his place. What was the heredity of so important a child?

His father was a Plantagenet who had inherited the powerful physique of that aggressive Angevin family as well as a slight cast in one eye and a liability to outbursts of ungovernable rage. As a young man, he and his private company of two hundred reckless boon companions had been the scourge of the countryside – they had sacrilegiously raided and maltreated the monks of Walsingham in Norfolk, one of the most sacred shrines in the kingdom, and on another occasion the young prince had ordered an inoffensive youth, casually met on the highway, to suffer the loss of an ear and an eye simply for his pleasure. There was more than a trace of what is now termed sadism in Edward I. True, the savage prince had later become the sincere Crusader and the great king, but his ill-tempered violence never left him, and his treatment of the family of Robert Bruce, of William Wallace and of his own son are blots on an otherwise brilliant escutcheon. Moreover, when his heir was born, the king was already a man of forty-five: such an age-difference would naturally make mutual understanding between father and son more difficult. And Edward I's great European reputation and national fame could be a handicap as well as a stimulus – it would not be easy for a son to emulate a father who as prince had defeated in battle the great Simon de Montfort, and who as

---

[1] John Stow, *Annales of England* (London, 1592), 202–3; A. J. Taylor *Caernarvon Castle and Town Walls*, H.M.S.O., 1969, 9–10; Sir Charles Peers in *History*, XXI (1937), 306–7; and cf *The History of the King's Works* (H.M.S.O., 1963), I, 369–95; J. G. Edwards in Procs. British Academy XXXII (1946), 43–52.

king had outgeneralled the Saracen, eliminated the native princes of Wales, who was to confiscate the Scottish Stone of Destiny for his English coronation throne, and who so often was to bring an unruly native baronage beneath the heel of his royal will. The very greatness of a father's reputation can be an unbearable weight on his sons.

Edward of Caernarvon's mother was Queen Eleanor of Castile. She was a Spaniard, the daughter of the king of Castile and Joanna of Ponthieu, and she had married 'The Lord Edward' at the age of ten in the great gloomy monastery of Las Huelgas on the hills above Burgos in northern Spain. She must have been a remarkable woman – she bore her husband thirteen children, she held his unswerving devotion throughout a long married life, she was the heroine of the legend that on crusade in the Holy Land she had saved her lord's life by sucking poison from a wound made by an assassin's dagger, and in her memory her grief-stricken husband was inspired to erect those graceful 'Eleanor Crosses' which marked the stages of her funeral procession from Nottinghamshire to Westminster, and to commission the superb effigy from William Torel for her resplendent tomb in the Abbey at Westminster.[1] But Eleanor's direct influence on Edward of Caernarvon can only have been through her Spanish blood – she left England with her husband when the prince was only two, and she died within fifteen months of their return just over three years later.

Of his grandmother, Eleanor of Provence, the widow of Henry III, Edward of Caernarvon may have had clearer and pleasant memories. She was the daughter of the count of Provence and sister to the queen of France, and had long lived down the unpopularity she had earned by her early patronage of foreign courtiers. Her son was devoted to her, and had lost a battle by over-keenness in taking vengeance on Londoners who had insulted her. On the death of Henry III, she had gracefully retired from court, and soon after the birth of Edward of Caernarvon she became a nun of the Order of Fontevrault in its English convent at Amesbury in Wiltshire. Judging by

[1] F. M. Powicke, *King Henry III and the Lord Edward* (Oxford, 1947), II, 733–4.

surviving letters[1] she nevertheless kept a kindly watch over her grandson's welfare, but she was over sixty when he was born and she died when he was only seven.

In his youth, Edward of Caernarvon had no brothers, but there is evidence that he was fond of his sisters, and especially of Elizabeth who was only two years his senior, and who, like himself, had been born in Wales, and of the Mary who early in life became a nun at Amesbury like her grandmother.

Edward's early boyhood was not over-supplied with the comforts of normal parental interest and family affections. His mother had died when he was very young, four of his sisters were married and away long before he reached manhood, and his father was forty-five years his senior, whose discipline became more violent as, disappointed and thwarted, he neared the end of his long and eventful life.

Little is known of the earliest years of Edward of Caernarvon. His first wet-nurse was a Mary Mawnsel who was probably Welsh. She soon fell ill at Rhuddlan, and was succeeded by Alice Leygrave, an English wet-nurse, who, with her relations, was to be well rewarded for her long service both to the baby Edward and later to his queen.[2]

The prince's doctor was Master Robert de Cysterne. On one occasion he was urgently needed to attend Edward at Windsor,[3] and he treated both Edward and his sister Margaret for tertian ague when the prince was nine. But all accounts agree that Edward grew up physically strong and handsome. 'Faire of body and grate of strengthe' says one; 'tall and strong, a fine figure of a handsome man' says another; and a herald poet described him at seventeen, as 'of a well proportioned and handsome person, of a courteous disposition and well-bred' and added that 'he managed his steed wonderfully well' and 'was desirous of finding an occasion to make proof of his strength'.[4]

Concerning Edward's book learning, or lack of it, there is less unanimity. His native language was, of course, Norman–French,

---

[1] *Ancient Correspondence*, Public Record Office, XVI, 151, 170.
[2] H. Johnstone, *Edward of Carnarvon 1284–1307* (Manchester, 1946), 9.
[3] H. Johnstone, *Letters*, 115.
[4] *Roll of Arms . . . Caerlaverock*, ed. T. Wright, Rolls Series, 1864, 18.

but he needed at least a working knowledge of two other languages – enough English to talk with his humbler subjects, and enough Latin to share in that European culture and diplomacy whose 'lingua franca' it was throughout the middle ages.[1] It is known that Edward owned books in French and in Latin, but that is no proof that he could or could not read them. He was to take his oath at his coronation in French although a Latin form was available,[2] but succeeding monarchs were also to take the oath in French 'so that what is the better understood may bear the richer fruit', but this may only mean that Edward's Latin was not as good as his French, and of that there need be no doubt.[3] On the other hand, there is a Latin poem quoted in the chronicles of the Elizabethan Fabyan which is there ascribed to Edward. But there is also a French version of this poem which existed as early as 1350, and whether Edward wrote either can now neither be proved nor disproved.[4] The conclusion must be that the prince was probably no scholar, but he was not expected to be. He nevertheless must have had the normal upbringing due to one of his rank and prospects, an education concerned chiefly with manners at court and table and with prowess in riding, hunting and jousting . . .

Edward's tutor and guardian was Sir Guy Ferre, and he could not have had a better.[5] Ferre was a soldier and courtier of long experience. He had served the prince's grandfather and grandmother, he had accompanied their younger son Edmund Crouchback on crusade to the Holy Land, he remained the honoured steward to Eleanor of Provence until her death, and he was well rewarded by Edward I. Sir Guy died at Durham in 1303 when he was on his way north to join a campaign against

[1] V. H. Galbraith, *The Literacy of the Medieval English Kings*, Procs. British Academy (London, 1935), 21.

[2] See below p. 56 and note 2.

[3] Walter Reynolds, *Register*, Lambeth, f. 218.

[4] R. Fabyan, *New Chronicles of England and France*, ed. Ellis, London, 1811, 430; P. Studer in *Modern Language Review*, XVI (1921), 34–46; A. Benedetti, *Nuovi Studi Medievali*, XIII (1924), 283; T. F. Tout, *Collected Papers* (Manchester, 1934), III, 189–90; for trans. see J. Harvey *The Plantagenets* (London, 1963), 148–54.

[5] H. Johnstone, *Edward of Carnarvon*, *op. cit.* 17. Ferre was Edward's 'magister', which meant 'moral tutor' or 'house-master' rather than a teacher or instructor.

the Scots. Prince Edward later attended the funeral mass in Durham cathedral for the soul of this chivalrous old man who had been his respected guardian for over eight vital years.

Sir Guy, as the herald-poet had noted, at least made his prince a competent horseman, and we know from other sources that Edward was an enthusiastic follower of the chase, and a keen breeder of horseflesh. It is from this time that we have the earliest-known English treatise on hunting – *Le Art de Venerie* – which was written by Edward's own huntsman,[1] and there is a letter extant which reveals Edward begging a stallion for his mares from his friend the archbishop of Canterbury.[2] Sir Guy must also have approved his pupil's enthusiasm for music – drum, pipe and trumpet were ever the correct accompaniment to majesty. But Edward's enthusiasm was more than merely orthodox. Throughout his life he was to be the keen patron of musicians and minstrels, and he took a pioneering interest in that early form of the violin which its Welsh exponents called the 'crwth'. There are records that a 'croudarius' was specially summoned to play for him at Windsor Castle, that he rewarded 'Roger le Croudere' for playing before him and his sister Elizabeth, and that he even sent one of his household – Richard the Rhymer – to Shrewsbury to learn how to play it.[3] On the other hand, neither Sir Guy nor conventional authorities generally approved of Edward's love of theatricals and buffoon-ery – it was said later with scorn by the orthodox that his friend Walter Reynolds chiefly owed his archbishopric to the fact that he was an accomplished actor and producer.[4]

In another important field Sir Guy certainly failed – he was unable to kindle in Edward any enthusiasm for those knightly exercises in the joust and the tourney which was expected of every conventional male aristocrat in the middle ages. A contemporary chronicler says sadly that if the prince 'had given to arms the labour that he expended on rustic pursuits, he

---

[1] A. Dryden (ed.), *The Art of Hunting by William Twick, Huntsman to Edward II* (Northampton, 1908).

[2] H. Johnstone, *Letters*, 82–3 and 97. Below p. 163.

[3] H. Johnstone, *Edward of Carnarvon, op. cit.* 64–5 and n 2; H. Johnstone, *Letters*, 114 and xiv–xlvi; P. A. Scholes, *The Oxford Companion to Music*, (Oxford, 1938), 223–43. See below p. 164.

[4] *Vita*, 45.

would have raised England aloft; his name would have re-sounded throughout the land',[1] and less sympathetic chroniclers complained bitterly that he forsook the normal pursuits of his peers and preferred to waste his time in the company of carters, diggers, ditchers, rowers, sailors, boatmen, and such rural craftsmen as thatchers and blacksmiths, and in the enjoyment of the mechanical arts and such undignified pursuits as bathing, rowing and swimming.[2]

Of Edward's moral stature there is also criticism. It is recorded that he was given to the company of harlots, that he could not keep a confidence, that he was carelessly extravagant, too much addicted to gambling and especially to that vulgar game of 'cross and pile' which is now called 'pitch and toss'.[3] But this kind of comprehensive disapproval was written much later to justify his fate, and need not be taken too literally. Strictly contemporary evidence did complain of Edward idling away his time in rural pursuits 'and other improper occupations' and there is the revealing backhanded compliment from the bishop of Worcester who noted that 'for once' he was behaving magnificently and 'contrary to his former custom getting up early in the morning'.[4] There is also a description of Edward's conduct at a later diplomatic conference with the French which proves that he could be energetic, eloquent and shrewd when he wished.[5] And there is general agreement that Edward grew up a good churchman who was regular in his devotion to such sacred shrines as Walsingham and Canterbury, and who was most generous in his endowment of the Dominicans near his favourite home at Langley in Hertfordshire.

Today it is difficult to obtain a clear view of a medieval prince's personality, but in the case of Edward of Caernarvon we obtain at least a few revealing glimpses. We read that he kept a camel in the stables of his Hertfordshire home, and that

---

[1] *Vita*, 40.

[2] *Flores Hist.*, III, 173. *Higden*, VIII, 292–9; *Knighton*, I, 407–8; *Tout, Place*, 9 note 2.

[3] *Vita*, 40 and *The Antiquarian Repertory*, II, 406; *Melsa*, II, 286; *Bridlington*, 91.

[4] cf. H. Johnstone in *E.H.R.*, XLVIII (1933), 264–7 and *Register of Thomas Cobham, bishop of Worcester*, (Worcester 1930), 97–8.

[5] cf. E. Pole Stuart in *E.H.R.*, XLI (1926), 412–15.

he took a lion with him on his campaigns and progresses.[1] And there is certainly amusing evidence of both wit and some literary ability in the letter he wrote as a young man of twenty-one to the count of Evreux – 'We send you a big trotting palfrey which can hardly carry its own weight, and some of our bandy-legged harriers from Wales who can well catch a hare, if they find it asleep, and some of our running dogs which go at a gentle pace – for well we know that you take delight in lazy days. And, dear cousin, if you want anything else from our land of Wales, we can send you plenty of wild lads, if you wish, who will know well how to teach breeding to the young heirs and heiresses of great lords.'[2] It is clear that Edward II's education produced a prince with several odd traits of character, but most of those which earned him the disapproval of his contemporaries would in no way disconcert a modern generation. At least Sir Guy Ferre was responsible for a personality and not a nonentity.

[1] H. Johnstone, *Edward of Carnarvon, op. cit.* 30, 86 and note 4; *C.D.S.*, 364, 366.
[2] H. Johnstone, *Letters,* 11.

Chapter 2

PRINCE
AND
HERITAGE

When he was only five years of age Edward of Caernarvon was
summoned to his first state function as heir to the throne. He
and his sisters travelled from the royal manor house at Langley
in Hertfordshire to Dover – the journey took a fortnight – to
join in the official welcome to their parents on their return from
a stay of just over three years abroad. During the next few years,
Edward frequently accompanied his father on his royal
progresses over the south of England, he went as far west as
Bristol to attend the wedding of his eldest sister Eleanor to the
count of Bar, whose lands were in the foothills of the Vosges, and
he also dutifully made an early pilgrimage of his own to the
shrine of St Thomas at Canterbury. His was a peripatetic
boyhood, but very early in his life he seems to have found in the
manor at Langley a congenial home which he was soon to be
able to call his own. The house was first lent to him by his
mother, who held it from Edmund earl of Cornwall. Langley
had large and well-filled stables; there was the pleasant River
Gade with its two water mills, one for corn and the other for
the fulling of cloth, there were vines and orchards, a well-
stocked deer park, and all the fascinations of farm and garden
together with the pleasure and excitement of planning alterations to architecture and décor – here was the ideal place
to give free rein to Edward of Caernarvon's odd taste for
rural pursuits and crafts. A century later its name was to
become King's Langley – a memorial to the fact that it had

by then become a favourite country residence of two ill-starred kings.[1]

In the thirteenth century, the marriage of the heir to the throne was his parent's very urgent responsibility and a matter of high diplomacy which could not be settled too early. Edward's father was not slow in planning his son's matrimonial future, and in the event it was to bring both of them into disastrous contact with their northern neighbours in Scotland. And if the relations between England and Scotland during the next thirty years are to be fully understood, it is necessary first to describe in some detail their condition as Edward of Caernarvon approached manhood.

The kingdom of Scotland was not yet clearly defined either in area or status. The Shetlands, the Orkneys, the Hebrides (and the Isle of Man), and Caithness were more Norse than Gaelic. West and north of the 'Highland Line' was almost a *terra incognita*, where bloody Celtic clan feuds never ceased, and no royal writ ever ran. In the south-west, Galloway and Argyll were comparatively untamed. The only fertile soil was in the east and south, where a very mixed population was subject to superimposed Anglo-Norman feudal lords, whose loyalties were compromised by the lordships they still retained in England. The Romans had left behind them no traces save the sites of their military outposts, which could be seen as far north as Dingwall, the line of the Antonine ditch and rampart between Forth and Clyde, and the more substantial ruins of the fortified wall which Hadrian had built between Bowness on the Solway Firth and Wallsend on the Tyne. But the Border was still an ill-defined no-man's land. In William the Conqueror's day his eldest son had built a New Castle to hold the eastern gateway, William himself had marched to the Firth of Tay to make the Scottish king 'his man', and his successor had built a second castle at Carlisle to guard the western approaches. But the whole of Northumberland remained disputed territory. In Stephen's reign, it had actually been ceded to Scotland's great

[1] *Inventory of Historical Monuments Commission* (Herts), 133–5; *Victoria County Histories* (Herts). II, 235–40; *Place-Names of Hertfordshire*, English Place Name Soc., XV, 34, 44, 91.

King David, but it had been recovered by Henry II who again made Scotland an English fief. When Richard Coeur de Lion was desperate for funds for his crusade to the Holy Land, he sold this feudal overlordship to William the Lion for hard cash, and the awkward question of English supremacy remained unresolved.

The inhabitants of the geographical area we now call Scotland probably numbered a mere scattered half million in Edward's day. They included Irish, Celtic Picts and Scots (who had originally come from Ireland), Norse, Anglo–Saxons, Normans, a few Flemish weavers in the south, and of course folk of very mixed blood. Gaelic was the spoken language of the Celtic peoples in the west and north, Norman French was the language of court and castle in the south and east, Latin was the 'lingua franca' of the literate and the clergy, and beneath the surface a Scottish Anglo-Saxon-Gaelic dialect was taking root and beginning to blossom into a vigorous literary vernacular.

There was still no defined centre. The earlier Scottish kings lay in their tombs on the sacred island of Iona whence, at the time when St Augustine was converting Kent, St Columba and St Ninian had despatched their missionaries to convert a very savage Scottish mainland. In the twelfth century, the Cistercians had arrived from the south to build their great churches as far north as Elgin, Beauly and Dornoch, but these were merely islands of early culture in a sea very close to paganism. The Stone of Destiny, on which it had become the custom to enthrone Scottish kings, was at Scone, just north of Perth. The strategic capital was Stirling, and Edinburgh was a castle superbly perched on a rock rather than a capital city, and there were very few towns of more than one or two thousand inhabitants. Agriculture was limited to the central lowlands and it was very primitive. Wealth was derived from cattle rearing – or stealing – and there was a growing trade in wool, fish and hides in exchange for wines, corn, cloth and spices between the small east-coast ports and Germany and Norway, which were as near to Aberdeen and Berwick as to the Thames. Scotland was on the whole a poor and turbulent land with wide areas of desolate moor and forested mountains where the elk, the bear and the wolf were still hunted, with no well-organized manorial system, no all-embracing ecclesiastical episcopal and parish organization, no mature governmental and legal machinery, and with a monarchy which in spite of at least two great kings was not yet sure of its own stability and permanence. Of true Scottish nationality there was of course little sign; there was only a loyalty to lord and locality, in the north a devotion to the clan, and everywhere a passion for sturdy independence which might one day make sound foundations for a unified nation state.[1]

Edward's England was not so near to the primitive. Its boundaries were more clearly defined, but the principality of Wales only included Anglesey, Snowdonia, Flint and what became Cardiganshire and Caermarthenshire – the rest of Wales as we know it was the private property of the Lords Marcher. The Palatinates, which had their own courts and councils and sent no representatives to the national assemblies save their magnates, included Durham under its bishop, the royal earldom of Chester which included most of Flintshire, and part of Shropshire. Lancaster, which was to become a full County Palatine fifty years later, was the earldom of Edmund Crouchback, the younger brother of Edward I and the ancestor of the royal house of Lancaster, and already very independent of central governance. Cornwall, with its privileged tin miners, was a separate royal appanage with its own Celtic language. Yet England 'bound in with the triumphant sea' was a political, ecclesiastical, and geographical entity. The Norman conquerors had superimposed a French-speaking aristocracy upon an Anglo-Saxon population whose civilization was not to be despised, and had forged the iron foundations of a unified nation-state. The Angevins had carried the process further and established a strong centralized monarchy and royal law. The Plantagenets had survived formidable baronial revolts, and, in spite of Magna Carta (which was very much a charter of baronial privileges), they had succeeded in creating an England which was respected, and sometimes feared, in Europe, which

[1] For Scottish affairs see G. W. S. Barrow, *Robert Bruce* (London, 1965) and E. M. Barron, *The Scottish War of Independence* (2nd edit.) (London, 1934), *passim*.

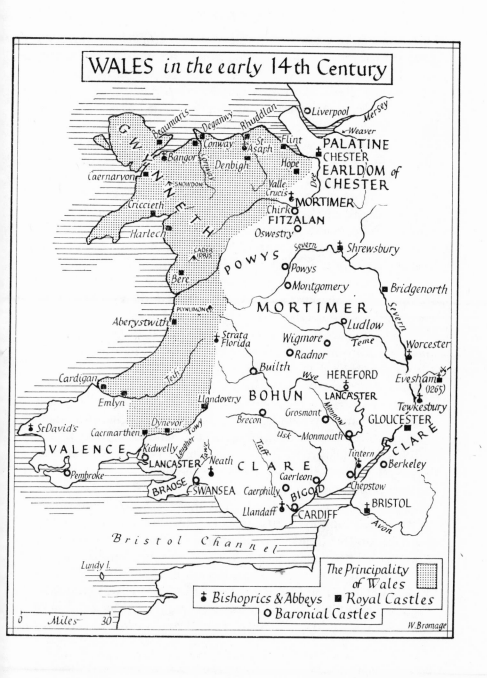

WALES *in the early* 14th Century

Liverpool
Mersey
Weaver
Deganwy
Rhuddlan
Beaumaris
Conway
St. Asaph
Flint
GWYNEDD
Bangor
Denbigh
Hope
PALATINE
CHESTER
EARLDOM of
CHESTER
Caernarvon
SNOWDON
Valle
Crucis
MORTIMER
Criccieth
Chirk
FITZALAN
Harlech
Oswestry
CADER
IDRIS
Severn
Shrewsbury
POWYS
Bere
Powys
Montgomery
Bridgenorth
PLYNLIMON
MORTIMER
Severn
Aberystwith
Ludlow
Strata
Florida
Wigmore
Teme
Worcester
Teifi
Radnor
Cardigan
Builth
Wye
HEREFORD
Evesham
(1265)
Emlyn
Llandovery
BOHUN
LANCASTER
Tewkesbury
St David's
Dynevor
Brecon
Grosmont
Monnow
GLOUCESTER
Caermarthen
Towy
Usk
Monmouth
CLARE
VALENCE
Kidwelly
Loughor
Taws
Neath
Taf
CLARE
Tintern
Pembroke
LANCASTER
Caerleon
Berkeley
BRAOSE
SWANSEA
Caerphilly
BIGOD
Chepstow
Llandaff
CARDIFF
BRISTOL
Avon

Bristol   Channel

Lundy I.

The Principality
of Wales
✝ Bishoprics & Abbeys   ■ Royal Castles
○ Baronial Castles

0   Miles   30

W. Bromage

had sent its princes and nobles to the Holy Land and its princesses to royal alliances in France, Burgundy, Spain and Germany, and which was linked to the culture now radiating from Rome, Paris, Burgundy and Flanders.

The English church had produced saints, philosophers as distinguished as Roger Bacon, Duns Scotus and Thomas Aquinas, and even the first (and only) English pope,[1] but, more important, it had its efficient administrators, and a system of bishoprics and parishes which covered the land, and stabilized rural boundaries which have lasted to the present day. The skill of English architects and builders was beginning to rival that of French masters whether they were building cathedrals, castles or palace halls. The cities of England were large and prosperous islands of freedom in an agricultural England whose feudal manorial system anchored the majority of the population to the soil. The ports of England carried on a trade 'from Gothland to Finisterre' which exchanged wool, cloth, hides, fish and minerals for the wines of France and all the luxuries of the great European trade fairs. The fleeces of English sheep and the cloth of English weavers were the main bases of a real economic prosperity. And, in spite of occasional setbacks, law and order were the acknowledged benefits of a centralized and efficient monarchy which, in a constant struggle with over-mighty subjects, was beginning to find valued support in the knights of the shires and the burgesses of the towns, and thus laying the foundations for future nationhood.

The population of England at the end of the thirteenth century is not easily estimated, but there is general agreement that it was probably a little over two and a half million – five times that of Scotland.[2] The language of the bulk of the people was that Anglo–Saxon, fertilized by additions from French and Latin, which was soon to blossom into the English of Chaucer and Langland. The language of court and castle was Norman–French, the official language of the clergy and the legal laity was of course L tin, and in Cornwall and in Wales ordinary

---

[1] The pope was Nicholas Breakspear, born at Langley, who in 1154 became Pope Adrian IV (d. 1159). See *D.N.B.* and W. Ullman in *Cambridge Historical Journal*, XI (1955), 233–52.

[2] M. McKisack, *The Fourteenth Century* (Oxford, 1959), 313.

people still spoke their local versions of the original Celtic language of the Britons.

But what was the daily lot of the ordinary people? It could certainly not be called a 'Merry England'. A contemporary abbot of Burton wrote that most of the populace 'owned nothing but their bellies', and soon Froissart, a shrewd French observer, was to remark on the 'great servage' of serf and villein which would finally burst into a catastrophic Peasants' Revolt. There were prosperous merchants and wealthy prelates, but there were thousands of discontented and needy apprentices, too many poor preachers, hordes of nomadic wayfarers and gangs of free-booting soldiery roaming the dangerous trackways between villages and towns. The lord of the manor in his castle or fortified manor-house might quail in the royal presence, but he was truly a despot in his own hall. There was law – but no police to enforce it, and every civilian carried his short sword or 'anlace', and was fully prepared to use it. Too often the life of the ordinary man was 'nasty, brutish and short'.

Yet there was a brighter side. In a hard world of serfdom and toil, the church had enabled all men to enjoy the freedom of sabbaths, and the many holy days of the many saints. In a world where the lord protected his private hunting with savage forest laws, there was still plenty of opportunity for rural sports, the rivalry of archery, the thrills of bear-baiting, and those rough ball games and mimic battles which delighted country yeomen and city apprentices alike. The manorial system was largely self-sufficient, and famine was rare. Already at Oxford there was the beginning of a university system which was to open the doors of palaces, cathedrals and courts to servants who owed their good fortune to their brains rather than their purses, their birth, or their brawn. There was a general respect for fine craftsmanship which expressed itself in the tradition of the 'just price' – a phrase which covered the quality of the product as well as the justice of the payment. Fine masons were vaulting and decorating great cathedrals; skilled glaziers were filling the great cathedral windows; devoted needlewomen were producing gorgeous tapestries for altars and vestments which were achieving a European fame; anonymous artists were covering the walls of village churches with frescoed sacred stories; minstrels were making music for lords and populace; actors were playing in those 'mysteries' which were the beginnings of our modern theatre; woodworkers were carving noble reredoses, amusing misericords and decorated bench ends; scribes and artists were producing brilliantly illuminated lay and clerical manuscripts; the shipwrights and sailors, whose tiny ships were conquering the Narrow Seas, were as traders and part pirates laying the foundations of English sea-power ... Here was the creation of an England which baron and serf, mayor and citizen, knight and yeoman, prelate and priest were beginning to think of as a land to which they owed their homage, their service, and soon if necessary their lives.[1]

And England already had a central government of long standing and of fixed abode. The twin cities of London and Westminster, at the centre of a road system which covered the country and went back as far as Roman times, situated at the first bridge on England's largest river and facing the Continent, had begun since the Conqueror's day to oust Winchester as the country's recognized capital. Here was the royal exchequer although it could still be moved to York when necessary. In Edward the Confessor's day the royal treasure had been stored in the royal bedroom, now the Exchequer barons were great civil servants in a great department of state. The king's justice was usually dispensed in the great palace hall at Westminster which has survived to our own day, and students of the law were beginning to meet in the lanes near the Templar's round church just west of the city of London's western gate. When the king wished to consult his council he summoned it usually to Westminster, and recently he had had occasion to summon men who were not just barons, but representatives of those knights and burgesses who were the leading officers of shires and towns. Nearly a hundred years before, King John had been forced to yield a charter of liberties to rebelling barons. That charter had since been confirmed; even the great Edward I was about to

[1] For English life in the Middle Ages, G. G. Coulton's many works are still authoritative, and so is the classic *English Wayfaring Life in the Middle Ages* by J. J. Jusserand. Mrs Jacquetta Hawkes estimates that the medieval peasant enjoyed fifty-two Sundays plus fifty-six Holy Days including of course the ten days at Christmas.

be forced to re-confirm it, and it was beginning to be seen as a statement of the rights of all free men. And outside London were many fair cities and prosperous ports, where civic freedom and liberties were as vital and as precious as they were in the capital. England as a whole was a unified community of communities, where every man save the outlaw knew and respected his obligations to other men whether organized in parishes, households, manors, shires, hundreds, gilds, crafts, moots, courts, councils or military and trading companies – and even the outlaws had their bands. It was a swarming, lively, vigorous, litigious, and prickly society, never quite sure whither it was going but always refusing to retreat. In relation to foreigners, and to all its neighbours, it was frequently liable to show aggression beyond its powers, but it was rightly jealous and proud of its own security and strength.

To a king as logically-minded and as ambitious as Edward I, the unification of the whole of Britain was a reasonable objective. By the time of Edward of Caernarvon's birth, the attempt to bring the Welsh to heel seemed to have succeeded. There now came a heaven-sent opportunity to find similar success north of the Scottish border.

In 1286, the able King Alexander III of Scotland had lamentably died after his horse had thrown him over the cliffs of the Forth when he was making a night-ride to visit his new queen, who was at Kinghorn. His heir was his granddaughter Margaret, then aged three, whose father was the king of Norway, and who is therefore known to history as the Maid of Norway. Edward I of England saw his chance – he immediately suggested a linking between the two monarchies. By a treaty sealed at Brigham, near Berwick, in March 1290, it was agreed that Edward of Caernarvon should marry the Maid of Norway, and so ensure the permanent alliance under one monarchy of an England and a Scotland which could each retain responsibility for its own internal affairs.[1] Preparations for the royal wedding went ahead, and proctors were actually appointed to contract the marriage on the young prince's behalf. A luxurious ship was

[1] Rymer I, 719–21, 738; J. Stevenson, *Documents illustrative of the History of Scotland* (Edinburgh, 1870), I, 105–11, 162–73.

sent by Edward to Norway to convey the Maid to England. In October, the tragic news arrived that the Maid of Norway had died in Orkney on her way to England, and that her body had been taken back to Bergen for burial in the cathedral there.[1] So was thwarted an excellent matrimonial project which, if consummated, might have anticipated the day when James VI of Scotland became James I of England, and so might have saved England and Scotland three hundred years of pointless strife. Scotland was cursed with a disputed succession, and Edward I had to look elsewhere for a wife for his son and heir.

Meanwhile, Scotland's dilemma was Edward's opportunity. In their difficulty, the Scottish barons were foolish enough to turn to Edward I for help, and in 1291 the English king took an army north, and, in exchange for a grudging admission that he was their 'sovereign lord', he agreed to act as the presiding judge at a full legal inquiry which was to decide between the rights of fourteen claimants to the vacant Scottish throne. In August, the inquiry opened at Berwick before twenty-four assessors from the English Council, forty nominees of John Balliol of Galloway, and forty of Robert Bruce of Annandale, which proves that these two were the only serious candidates.[2] It was a remarkable display of legal fencing, but the fascinating details of the arguments are outside the scope of this study. The inquiry – known as the Great Cause – was not completed until over a year later, and, on 17 November 1292, Edward I announced that, in accordance with the strict and now recognized rules of primogeniture, the heir to the throne of Scotland was John Balliol.[3] On St Andrew's Day, 1292, Balliol was crowned on the Stone of Destiny at Scone. He was the great-grandson of David I's youngest son, while Bruce was a grandson; but Balliol's mother was the elder sister of Bruce's mother and Balliol therefore had the better claim – and no one could seriously dispute it.

Unfortunately for Scotland, John Balliol was no match for

[1] A. O. Anderson, *Early Sources of Scottish History* (Edinburgh, 1922), II, 695.

[2] See F. Palgrave, *Documents and Records – The History of Scotland* (Edinburgh, 1870), I, No. 108.

[3] For the 'Great Cause' see *Rymer*, I, 762–84 and *Rishanger*, 234–368.

1 Eleanor of Castile, mother of Edward II

2 Margaret of France, Edward's stepmother

the aggression of Edward I. He is known to Scottish history as 'Toom Tabard' which means 'Empty Jacket' or 'King Nobody', and he had readily paid his homage to Edward. Edward treated him with a legalism near to contempt – he actually summoned him to feudal military service in France. In 1295 even 'Toom Tabard' at last resisted Edward's increasing encroachments; he renounced his allegiance, and initiated that covenant with England's French enemies which later became the celebrated and fateful 'Auld Alliance'.

In March 1296, Edward's armies again entered Scotland. The Anglo–Scottish lords again found themselves torn between competing allegiances. When in 1204 King John had lost nearly all his French possessions, he had unwittingly done England a great service. In future, magnates who held lands in both England and France had to decide where their allegiance lay; they had to become either wholly English or wholly French. Unfortunately there was now no similar ill-wind to blow some good over the Scottish border. Over eighty of the Scottish lords rendered homage to Edward at Wark in Northumberland, and they included the Robert Bruce who was the grandson of Balliol's rival and destined to usurp 'Toom Tabard's' empty throne. Balliol, on hearing this grievous news, immediately confiscated the Bruce's Scottish estates and transferred them to his own brother-in-law, John Comyn of Badenoch, who was a leading Scottish lord. Scotland was hopelessly divided in the face of the invader.

The first action of Edward's new invasion was to make an example of the city of Berwick. The ruthless slaughter, destruction and rapine meted out by Edward's soldiery were never forgotten, and Berwick never fully recovered.[1] Its trading supremacy was lost to Edinburgh, and Edward attempted to re-found the ruined town as he had rebuilt the 'bastides' in Gascony, Winchelsea on the south coast, and Caernarvon in North Wales, as an English headquarters staffed by English burgesses for the future administration of Scotland. There followed a bloody battle near Dunbar in which Balliol's army was routed by an English army which actually included contingents from the Bruce family and other Scottish lords. Many

[1] *Lanercost*, 134–5; *Guisborough*, 277.

Scots were slain and many taken prisoner for ransom, and, although Balliol himself escaped from the battlefield, his flight ended ignominiously when he surrendered his kingdom and his crown to England at Brechin in Angus on 10 July.[1] 'Toom Tabard', together with the Scottish regalia and the Stone of Destiny,[2] was sent to England, where, after a reasonably comfortable lodging in the Tower of London and in Hertford Castle, 'King Nobody' was finally allowed to retire to France, and eventually to his ancestral estates where he died in comfortable dishonour some seventeen years later.

Edward I, meanwhile, took his armies as far north as Elgin and in August 1296 returned to Berwick, where his officials were still compiling the proofs of Scotland's disgrace – those 'Ragman Rolls' which record the homage of hundreds of the Scottish nobility, gentry and clergy.[3] The Stone of Destiny was soon to be built into a new Coronation Chair at Westminster Abbey, on which English monarchs have been crowned ever since, and of which Edward of Caernarvon was to be the first English occupant.[4] Every important Scottish castle was garrisoned by Englishmen, only the Comyn family were keeping alive a show of resistance, and one William Wallace's name was certainly not on any Ragman Roll – he was about to upset English equanimity with a vengeance. The English conquest of Scotland was not as complete as it seemed – Edward I had to fight five campaigns in Scotland during the last decade of his long life, and there his son was to take his first lessons in active military service.

[1] *Guisborough*, 277–80. Stevenson, *op. cit.* II, No. 372.

[2] M. Dominica Legge in *S.H.R.*, XXXVIII, 109–13.

[3] *C.D.S.*, II, No. 823; T. Thomson (ed.), *Instrumenta Publica . . . homagiis Scotorum 1291–1296* (Bannatyne Club, 1834). 60–174.

[4] Edward's new chair was made in 1307 and decorated by Walter of Durham, the King's Painter. cf. A. P. Stanley, *Historical Memorials of Westminster Abbey* (London, 1882), 55–9 and L. E. Tanner, *Westminster Abbey and The Coronation Service* (London, 1953), 291.

Chapter 3

APPRENTICESHIP

The ambitions of Edward I were not confined to Wales and Scotland. The aggressions and trickery of Philip IV of France gave him the excuse to tempt fortune across the Channel, and it was as part of a bold foreign policy designed to encircle France that Edward, in January 1297, sealed a treaty which provided for the marriage of Edward of Caernarvon to Philippa the daughter of Guy of Dampierre, count of Flanders, or failing her, to her sister.[1] In early February 1298, proctors for the formal sworn betrothal met Edward at Walsingham. Meanwhile, the king had planned a pincer attack on France with himself leading one army from Flanders and the constable, Humphrey de Bohun, earl of Hereford, and the marshal, Roger Bigod, earl of Norfolk, leading a second army from Gascony. This complex strategy needed money and the co-operation of both the Constable and the Marshal, whose traditional positions were alongside the person of their king. In a parliament at Bury St Edmunds in November 1296, the knights of the shire and the burgesses were co-operative, but the two earls were recalcitrant in their objections to separation from their king, and the clergy, under their obstinate archbishop Winchelsey, claimed that the papal Bull *Clericis Laicos* (24 February 1296) forbade the payment of civil taxes from church revenues unless expressly approved by the pope. The details of the ensuing crisis do not concern the history of Edward of Caernarvon except that, on 14 July 1297, the quarrel was settled at a spectacular public ceremony staged at Westminster. Outside King Rufus' great hall, a special dais had been erected, and from it the king made a tearful speech of apology and an

[1] This marriage had been first suggested in June 1294, but French opposition had delayed its fruition. *Rymer*, I, 803.

impassioned appeal for help in his foreign adventuring. Edward of Caernarvon was present, and the old king went on to hint that in the service of his people he might himself die. He therefore demanded that all the magnates present should there and then publicly swear fealty to his son as his heir and their future lord.[1] It was a moving occasion for an impressionable thirteen-year old.

Well content with what seemed a propaganda success, the king sailed for Flanders in August leaving his son as his regent in England. But the royal peace of mind was ill-founded to the point of rashness. He left behind him a country very near to civil war, a new threat from a resurgent Scotland, and a boy regent while the country's best fighting men were dispersed between Gascony, Flanders and Scotland.

The revolt in Scotland had begun even before Edward sailed. It added three famous names to the roll of Scotland's national heroes – William Wallace, Andrew Murray, and Robert Bruce.

Of Wallace's origins there is no certainty. He was not the 'man from nowhere' his detractors have alleged – almost certainly he came from one of the knightly Border families who acknowledged the noble James the Stewart as their feudal lord. But if, indeed, he was 'of gentle blood', as his eulogists have claimed, the adjective 'gentle', in another sense, is a grave misnomer for so savage a freebooter. In May 1297, Wallace had murdered William Hesilrig, the English sheriff of Lanark,[2] and he had followed up this signal for general revolt by a daring and successful raid in conjunction with Sir William Douglas on the English justiciar's headquarters at Scone.

Andrew Murray was the heir of Sir Andrew Murray, lord of the Great Glen. He had been imprisoned in Chester Castle after the English victory at Dunbar, but had escaped to lead a revolt from the north which swept the English invaders from Inverness, Elgin and Banff,[3] and by August of 1297 he was able

[1] *Flores Hist.*, III, 295 and *Guisborough*, 123.

[2] J. Stevenson, *Documents Illustrative of Sir William Wallace, his Life and Times* (Maitland Club, 1841), 191; *Scalacronica*, 123.

[3] *C.D.S.*, II, nos. 921, 2 and 3.

to join forces with Wallace from the south in an attack upon the strategic centre of Scotland – Stirling Castle.

Robert Bruce, the grandson of Balliol's chief rival at the Great Cause, had hitherto fought for his English overlord Edward even against some of his own Scottish peers. He was now about twenty-two years of age, earl of Carrick, heir to many acres in Annandale and the south-west, and at last certain on which side he wished to stand. It was not an easy decision to make. He owed much to Edward I who had restored his father to his Scottish estates, and, like many of the Scottish lords, he had ancestral, feudal and personal ties which bound him closely to allegiances and properties south of the Border. His latest biographer[1] suggests that the surprising explanation, given by the chronicler Walter of Guisborough, that Bruce joined the Scots because he was a Scotsman, might be the simple truth.[2] However, Bruce's first efforts for his new allies were neither distinguished nor vigorous – his friends in the south-west capitulated, and, although he himself did not surrender, the struggle was left to the more aggressive methods of Murray and Wallace.

On 11 September 1297, the English occupation forces, under Edward's lieutenant in Scotland John de Warenne, earl of Surrey, and the treasurer Hugh Cressingham, were decisively defeated by Murray and Wallace in a battle near Stirling Bridge.[3] Warenne escaped but Cressingham was slain, and the 'gentle' Wallace had the corpse flayed, and its skin tanned and cut into small pieces as tokens of victorious revolt to stimulate wider resistance to the English occupation. The defeat of the English was due entirely to the folly of Warenne in sending mounted knights two by two over a long narrow bridge in the face of a ruthless, brave and well-positioned army of spearmen. It was the first time that the English had suffered a major defeat at the hands of Scotsmen, it was a victory of intelligently-led humble infantry over feudal, mounted knights, and it was the

[1] See G. W. S. Barrow, *Bruce, op, cit. passim.* The theme expressed in his subtitle, '*and the Community of the Realm of Scotland*', is less convincing than his admirable picture of the Bruce himself.

[2] *Guisborough*, 295.

[3] C. Oman, *A History of The Art of War in the Middle Ages* (New York, 1924), II, 75–7; *C.D.S.*, II, p. xxx; *Guisborough* 300–3.

victory of a new popular Scottish national spirit over the professional chivalry of the foreigner. Unfortunately for the Scots, young Andrew Murray was severely wounded in the battle and died two months later. While Bruce was ineffective in the south-west, Wallace and his borderers followed up their victory near Stirling with a series of brutal and devastating raids across the Border which the English regency could not prevent, and 'the praise of God ceased in every church and monastery from Newcastle-on-Tyne to Carlisle'.[1] Towards the end of the year, Wallace himself, in the name of captive King John assumed the responsibility of leader of the Scottish 'community of the realm'. But his triumph, spectacular as it was, was destined to be short-lived – in the New Year news arrived that Edward I was returning from Flanders specifically to bring the rebel Scots to heel.

The regency of the thirteen-year-old Edward of Caernarvon had lasted a mere seven months, but they were months of crisis and strain. Edward, of course, had only been a figurehead. The actual government of the kingdom had been in the hands of a regency council of three earls, three barons and four ecclesiastics, of whom the most effective was Walter Langton, bishop of Lichfield and treasurer of the Exchequer. Even before the king's departure for Flanders, the barons had presented him with a long list of their grievances, known as the 'Monstraunces', and the regency councillors had been left with the responsibility of meeting these grievances as best they could. The result was the celebrated 'Confirmation of the Charters' promulgated for the first time on 12 October 1297.[2] The Great Charter and the Charter of the Forest re-enacted by Edward's father were solemnly reiterated, the right to levy taxes of all kinds without consent was specifically abjured, and the word 'consent' was further defined as involving the 'will and assent of the church, the earls, barons, knights, burgesses and other free men of the kingdom'. It was a spectacular royal surrender which Edward was compelled to repeat three times before (on 14 February

[1] *Guisborough*, 303–7.
[2] See J. G. Edwards, '*Confirmatio Cartarum and baronial grievances in 1297*' in *E.H.R.*, LVIII (1943), 147–71 and 273–300 and H. Rothwell in *E.H.R.*, LX (1945), 16–35, 177–91, 300–15.

1301) the final 'confirmation' was conceded; but Edward was eventually to have the last word.[1]

It was a crisis which had come very close to civil war. The two recalcitrant earls – Bigod and Bohun – had taken their forces armed to meet the regency council at London, where Prince Edward had been sent so that he might find safety 'within the walls'.[2] The earls were therefore specifically pardoned, and the king, who was at Ghent and in close touch with his council throughout the negotiations, confirmed the regency's actions by letters patent on 5 November. Edward of Caernarvon had been compelled to witness his father apologizing publicly to his subjects; he himself had been the instrument of a prodigious victory for baronial privileges and liberties. He had experienced some of the risks of leadership when he was confined within the fortress of London in expectation of armed rebellion and, in reply to the raids of William Wallace over the Border, his regency council was summoning armies to an expedition into Scotland which promised him a first taste of warfare. His short regency had been perhaps overfull of incident and experience.

On 14 March 1298, Edward I arrived back in England after a singularly fruitless Flemish adventure which left him an exasperated and ageing man. Now Prince Edward was able to step off the public stage for a couple of years, and enjoy what was

---

[1] The following is a calendar of the various 'Confirmations':

July 1297.	The '*Monstraunces*' of the Barons' grievances.
12 Oct. 1297.	Confirmation of the Charters with 6 additional articles by the regency.
5 Nov. 1297.	Confirmed by the King at Ghent.
1299.	A clause 'saving the rights of the crown' was added but had to be withdrawn.
6 Mar. 1300.	Twenty '*Articuli super Cartas*' issued.
14 Feb. 1301.	Final version authorized by parliament at Lincoln.
29 Dec. 1305.	Pope Clement V absolves Edward from his promises. *Rymer* I, 978.

For the 6 articles see W. Stubbs, *Select Charters*, 9th edit. (Oxford, 1913), 493–4 which refers to them as *De Tallagio non concedendo* (and which was subsequently quoted as a Statutum in the preamble to the Petition of Right in 1628) but are called by *Guisborough* '*Articuli inserti in Magna Carta*', see *C.M.H.*, VII, 410.

[2] *Guisborough*, 308–9.

left of his youth. It is at this period that a fateful name for ever associated with that of Edward of Caernarvon first appears in the records. During the Flemish expedition, a certain 'Perrot de Gaveston' was paid wages by the king for military service rendered from August to November 1297. His father was an Arnaud de Gabaston, who had fought for Edward I in the early part of his reign and had been taken prisoner by the French. In the previous year he had managed to escape, and he had promptly rejoined the king in England, possibly with his young son. Little is known of this Arnaud except that his reputed tomb is in Winchester cathedral. His family came from the Gascon village now called Gabaston which is a few miles north-east of Pau in Béarn, and they were of old and knightly stock. His son's wages began with the start of the Flemish campaign, and he apparently distinguished himself because he was appointed squire, or 'armiger', in the royal household, and on returning to England was made one of the ten *pueri in custodia* who were official companions in the household of Prince Edward. An anonymous chronicler, writing about thirty years later, relates what happened – 'And when the king's son saw him he fell so much in love that he entered upon an enduring compact with him. Whatever the precise interpretation of this comment may be, this friendship between an English prince and a Gascon squire was soon to dominate the domestic politics of England.[1]

Meanwhile, the failure of the Flemish alliance affected other royal plans. The projected marriage of Edward of Caernarvon with a daughter of the disappointing count of Flanders was abandoned, and arrangements were begun for a double marriage alliance with France which obtained the support of the pope. On 19 June 1299, a treaty was sealed at Montreuil by which the sixty-year-old widower Edward I was to marry the seventeen-year-old Margaret, sister of Philip IV of France, while Edward

[1] There are two biographies of Gaveston – M. Dimitresco, *Pierre de Gavaston, Sa Biographie et son Rôle* (Paris, 1898), and W. F. Dodge, *Pierre Gaveston* (London, 1899); but both are inadequate. See therefore *British Archaeological Assoc. Journal*, XII (1856), 94 and XV (1858), 125–32; *Sussex Archaeological Collections*, II, 96–7; G. L. Haskins in *Speculum*, XIV (1939), 73–81; H. Johnstone, *Edward of Carnarvon, op. cit.* 42–3.

of Caernarvon was to marry Isabella, Philip's daughter. On 4 September 1299, Edward I's second marriage was celebrated with great magnificence in Canterbury Cathedral.[1] Young Edward of Caernarvon now had a second mother young enough to be his sister, to whom he soon became warmly attached, and the prospect of a brilliant marriage with a king's daughter. At the time of their betrothal the prince was fifteen and the princess eight years old.

The king's first concern on returning home had been to meet the threat from William Wallace and the marauding Scots. On 22 July 1298, he totally defeated Wallace at the battle of Falkirk, and the Scottish hero was lucky to escape the slaughter[2] – Wallace was next heard of in France where he was unsuccessfully seeking aid from the French court and from the pope. The young Edward had played no part in this campaign – he had been left to enjoy his country manor at Langley, and to sow a few wild oats in Windsor and London. Glimpses of his life at this time can be seen in his surviving wardrobe accounts. His bargemaster was one Absalom of Greenwich, and the Thames was his usual highway between Windsor and the Tower. He was fond of betting and dicing, but he was also mindful of his duties to the church and her saints. He went on pilgrimage to Canterbury and made generous offerings at the national shrines. It was a normal and happy-go-lucky period of his life, and it did not last long.[3] By the early summer of the following year (1300) he was on his way north to join his father and experience warfare for the first time.

The armies moved slowly, and both father and son visited Bury St Edmunds on their way. The famous abbey's chronicler recorded that Edward stayed a week longer than his father, and 'became our brother in chapter. The magnificence of the abbey and the frequent recreations of the brethren pleased him greatly. Every day, moreover, he asked to be served with a monk's portion such as the brothers take in refectory.'[4] It is

[1] *Rymer*, I, 906–7; *Walsingham*, I, 79.

[2] C. Oman, *op. cit.* II, 78–80.

[3] H. Johnstone, *Edward of Carnarvon, op. cit.* 45.

[4] *Chronicle of Bury St Edmunds* ed. and trans. A. Gransden (London, 1964), xxxiii and 157.

31

a pleasant and rare anecdote of a prince who never lacked detractors.

After a march through Lincolnshire, the west riding of Yorkshire, Durham, and over the Pennines to Penrith, the army reached Carlisle on 25 June. This was a major expedition comprising perhaps 3,000 mounted men-at-arms and large numbers of infantry, and it was intended to attack that south-west corner of Scotland, where both the Bruce family and the Balliol family had their main Scottish lands and whence Wallace had found much of his support. It turned out to be an indecisive and disappointing foray, because the Scots wisely avoided battle. On the other hand, the heir to the English throne had his first experience of siege warfare and of actual fighting. At the siege of Caerlaverock Castle, which guarded the estuary of the river Nith, he watched huge siege engines hurling their stones against the walls. He himself was put in command of the English rearguard with veterans of his father's campaigns to give him support and advice, and, in a brisk if pointless skirmish with a Scottish force under the earl of Buchan, he acquitted himself well. The siege of Caerlaverock was over in five days, but the king's forces had penetrated as far as Wigtown and found no enemies to fight – they retreated to New Abbey on the Nith, where on 27 August, Archbishop Winchelsey was waiting to deliver a message to the king from the pope which deplored Edward's Scottish policy. The king's ferocious answer betrayed the strained temper of an ageing man 'By the blood of God . . . I will defend my right so long as the breath of life sustains my body.' For over two months longer the armies stayed over the Border, a final tour of inspection was made at the end of October, and on 16 November the English turned for home.[1] Edward of Caernarvon's first excursion in arms had earned the enthusiasm of at least one chronicler,[2] and it was not the prince's fault that the results were so disappointing. It may have been on this expedition that his friendship with Peter of Gaveston ripened – Peter was paid wages for services throughout the campaign.

[1] For this campaign see *Rishanger*, 439–53 and T. Wright, *Roll of Arms*, *op. cit. passim*, and H. Johnstone, *Edward of Carnarvon*, *op. cit.* 49 note 2.
[2] T. Wright, *Roll of Arms*, *op. cit.* 18.

The English forces had withdrawn as usual with the onset of winter. Edward spent a week at his beloved Langley before he represented his father at a special ceremony held on 12 January 1301, at the Augustinian priory at Ashridge in Buckinghamshire. There the body of Edmund earl of Cornwall and cousin to the king, who had died while the two Edwards were in Scotland, was finally laid to rest.[1] After the funeral, the prince rode away to join his father at the parliament then in session at Lincoln – it was to be a momentous occasion.

On 7 February 1301, a royal charter conferred upon Edward of Caernarvon a very impressive endowment.[2] He was granted as prince of Wales all the royal lands in Wales, together with the palatinate earldom of Chester with all its wide appurtenances. It was a generous and flattering bequest, and proves that at this time the father was well satisfied with his son's progress – it may have been the reward for his promising conduct during the Caerlaverock campaign. The Welsh bequest comprised the whole of Anglesey, Snowdonia, all north Wales from the city of Chester to the estuary of the Dyfi, and the lands which are now Cardiganshire and Caermarthenshire. The earldom of Chester included many castles and manors all over England as well as the valuable palatinate itself. The remainder of what is now Wales was in the undisputed possession of the fierce and independent Lords Marcher, but the prince's new patrimony included some of the greatest and most up-to-date castles in the land, excellent ports, lead mines and salt industries of great value, and a reserve of hardy mountain soldiery equipped with that long-bow which was soon to revolutionize European warfare.

The new prince of Wales left Lincoln to undertake a tour of his Welsh estates, and to receive the homage now due to him. He was kept busy with these ceremonies at Flint, Hope, Ruthin, Rhuddlan, and Conway in April, while several great English lords did homage to him for their Welsh lands at Kenilworth in May.

In April 1302 the manor of Langley had lapsed to the crown on the death of Edmund of Cornwall, and the king now granted

[1] L. M. Midgley in *T.R.H.S.*, 1942, pp. vii–xvii.
[2] *Cal. Pat. Rolls 1292–1301*, 576.

it to Edward. It was a valuable and much-appreciated acquisition, and since the prince, as far back as 1290, had inherited the County of Ponthieu and Montreuil from his mother, Queen Eleanor, it is clear that he was not ungenerously treated.[1] On the other hand, these endowments did not give the prince much real independence. Ponthieu, for example, had been handed over by his father to the care of the Frescobaldi of Florence, who continued to control it until 1308, and even the prince's freedom to appoint his own officers was severely limited and his expenditure controlled by the royal officials. He might now have additional means for occasionally rewarding his friends, but there were still not enough revenues to enable him to 'live of his own' without help from the royal exchequer, and the rigid control of his father and his father's ministers was eventually to lead to much unpleasantness.

For the next four years, however, both the king and the prince were harmoniously and heavily involved in the Scottish war. It was in exchange for baronial and feudal support at the parliament of Lincoln (February 1301) that the final version of yet another Confirmation of the Charters had been agreed, and the king was thus freed to make yet another attempt to subdue the Scots. The invasion of 1301 was to be two-pronged. The king was to take the larger part of the army over the Border from Berwick, while the prince was to have independent command of the remainder in an attack on the west from Carlisle. The prince's father hoped that 'the chief honour of taming the pride of the Scots should fall to his son',[2] and he therefore gave the prince the help of the elderly and experienced Henry de Lacy, earl of Lincoln, of Richard FitzAlan, earl of Arundel, and of three younger earls – Ralph de Monthermer, earl of Gloucester, Humphrey de Bohun, earl of Hereford, Thomas, earl of Lancaster – and also of a number of the prince's other contemporaries who were also his vassals in Cheshire and Wales. Peter of Gaveston, one of the royal wards, was also assigned to the prince's 'meinie', and Walter Reynolds, now the prince's

[1] For Ponthieu see H. Johnstone, *County of Ponthieu 1279–1307* in *E.H.R.*, XXIX (1914), 435–52.
[2] *CDS*. II no. 1191; G. W. S. Barrow, *Bruce, op. cit.* 170.

treasurer, was also with his young master – both were destined for distinction later. The prince's army was large, well organized and well equipped – the great values of many of the leaders' 'destriers' are in the records – and substantial reinforcements were due to arrive from Ireland once the Border was crossed, while useful supplies of Irish victuals were to be delivered to Skinburness near Carlisle and to a port on the Isle of Arran.

In spite of such careful preparations the campaign was again a disappointment. The king marched up Tweeddale and down Clydesdale to take the important castle of Bothwell (just south of Glasgow), which commanded the routes from the north to the south-west. The prince traversed the south-west from Annandale to Wigtown and up to Ayr. But, as the Lanercost chronicler put it, the Scots under the guardian Sir John de Soulis, did not dare to fight with either army but 'fled as in the previous year', and, as another chronicler has it, 'as none of the Scots would resist them, they achieved nothing glorious or praiseworthy'.[1] An inconclusive campaign ended by king and prince concentrating at Linlithgow for their winter quarters, where negotiations were begun for a truce. On 26 January 1302, a nine months' truce was agreed.[2] It was now that the rebel earl of Carrick, Robert Bruce, whose castle at Turnberry had held out until the previous September, deserted to the English. It was the beginning of a somewhat sordid chapter in the early life of the man who was to become the creator of Scottish nationalism. The submission of Robert Bruce may probably have been due to the news from Rome that John Balliol had been transferred from papal to French tutelage in his ancestral castle of Bailleul, and to the rumour that Philip IV of France was sending him to Scotland supported by a French army. The Bruce had nothing to look for from 'Toom Tabard', and might even lose his lands and his titles at his hands. The instrument of Bruce's submission to Edward therefore ensured Bruce's rights, and, in any case of dispute, decreed that Edward's courts would deal justice. If to Scots this is a blot on the escutcheon of their

[1] *Lanercost*, 172; *Flores Hist.*, III, 109.
[2] *C.D.S.*, II, no. 1282.

hero, to the English it was a solitary plume to grace Edward I's battered helm.[1]

It was again no fault of Prince Edward's that this Scottish campaign of 1301 was so inglorious. He had done all that could have been expected of him by his illustrious father, and this in spite of some touch of illness – his physician had hurried to London for 'certain matters required for the prince's body'.[2] His friend Gaveston, too, had needed medical attention – he was ordered to stay at Knaresborough to recuperate – and it may be that both had suffered from campaigning in what was recorded as appalling weather. Both father and son left Scotland at the end of February 1302, and they were not to return until over a year later.

This short interlude of peace found the prince taking his full part in affairs of state. In March, the chronicles say, 'the lord Edward held parliament with the magnates of England at London on behalf of King Edward his father',[3] and in the autumn he was present at a full parliament which included representatives of the shires and towns, and which urged the king to press on with measures to quell the Scottish rebels as soon as the truce expired. But the prince's wardrobe accounts give some intriguing glimpses of more personal affairs. His 'court' offered official receptions to distinguished visitors, his 'council' was busy with the affairs of his new earldom of Chester, the miners of his Welsh lands called for advice from German miners, and the seneschal of Ponthieu presented his accounts. The prince now left his Langley Manor for a time and spent most of December and January at South Warnborough in Hampshire, where his friend Sir Roger Pedwardine had his manor. From there he sent a gold ring set with a great ruby as a New Year present to Queen Margaret, and there he enjoyed the 'interludes' of actors from Windsor. He was a regular attendant at mass, a normal giver of alms on the appropriate occasions, and as fond of dicing as any other young noble of the day. His purchase of an illuminated life of Edward

[1] E. L. G. Stones in *S.H.R.*, XXXIV, 122–34.
[2] *C.D.S.*, II, No. 1249.
[3] *Ann. Lond.*, 127.

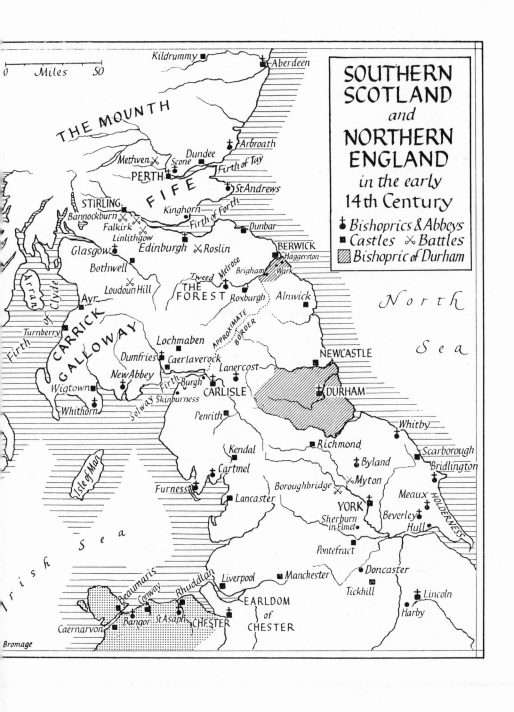

SOUTHERN SCOTLAND and **NORTHERN ENGLAND** in the early 14th Century

✝ Bishoprics & Abbeys
■ Castles ⤬ Battles
▨ Bishopric of Durham

0 *Miles* 50

THE MOUNT

Kildrummy ■   Aberdeen ✝■

✝ Arbroath

Methven ⤬   Dundee ■
Scone   Firth of Tay
PERTH   FIFE   St Andrews ✝

STIRLING   Kinghorn   Firth of Forth
Bannockburn ⤬   Dunbar ■
Falkirk ⤬   Linlithgow
Glasgow ✝   Edinburgh ■   Roslin ⤬   BERWICK ■
Bothwell ■   Haggerston
Loudoun Hill ⤬   Tweed   Melrose ✝   Brigham   Wark ■
THE FOREST   Roxburgh   Alnwick ■
Ayr ■
CARRICK   Lochmaben ■   APPROXIMATE BORDER
Turnberry ■   GALLOWAY   Dumfries ✝   Caerlaverock ■
New Abbey ✝   Lanercost ✝   NEWCASTLE ■
Wigtown ■   Firth   Burgh ✝   DURHAM ✝
Whithorn ✝   Skinburness   CARLISLE ✝
Solway   Penrith ■   Whitby ✝

Isle of Man   Kendal ■   Richmond ✝   Scarborough ■
Cartmel ✝   Byland ✝   Bridlington ✝
Furness ✝   Myton ⤬
Boroughbridge ⤬   Meaux ✝
Lancaster ■   YORK ✝   HOLDERNESS
Sherburn   Beverley ✝
in Elmet   Hull ✝

Irish Sea   Pontefract ■

Liverpool ■   Manchester ■   Doncaster ●
Beaumaris ■   Rhuddlan ■   Tickhill ■   Lincoln ✝
Conway ■   EARLDOM   Harby ●
Caernarvon ■   Bangor ✝   St Asaph ✝   of
CHESTER ✝   CHESTER

Bromage

North Sea

the Confessor at this time might give the lie to the subsequent
tradition that he was illiterate, save that he might have admired
the illuminations without necessarily being able to read the
text. And so academic an exercise was in contrast to the purchase
of a lion, complete with its chain, collar, keeper and cart, to
accompany him on his travels in war and in peace. Minstrels
entertained him, and there was 'sport in the water' – in spite of
the fact that it was only February. And in early March, the
prince was once again busy with preparations for war. He was
inspecting tents in Holborn, and supervising their emblazon-
ments. He was buying horses and saddlery, new crossbows and
longbows, banners with his own arms and the arms of St
Edward, St Edmund and St George, gold pennons for his
trumpeters, swords, swordbelts and scabbards, bascinets, caps
of iron, helms, and the gauntlets, cuisses, poleyns and jambs
which were now supplementing the ancient protection of
chain mail.[1]

All available men and supplies were to be at Berwick by the
end of May (1303). But on 24 February an English force
commanded by Edward's lieutenant in Scotland, Sir Thomas
Segrave, had been surprised and cut to pieces at Roslin, just
south of Edinburgh, by rebels under John Comyn, the younger,
of Badenoch and Simon Frazer of Oliver Castle. Segrave was in
Scottish hands for a time, and it was rumoured that William
Wallace was again in the field.[2] The effect on the king was to
stimulate still greater efforts to force a final answer to his
Scottish problems. Urgent preparations included the pre-
fabrication of three floating bridges, which were transported to
the Forth by sea so that the army might cross the firths of Forth
and Tay directly, and by-pass Stirling Castle on their way
north. The prince left London on 13 March for Scotland, and
he and his father duly reached Roxburgh by mid-May. There,
the good news arrived that, by a treaty sealed at Paris,[3] the
French were to keep out of the struggle and arrangements for
the eventual marriage between the prince and Isabella were
to continue.

[1] See H. Johnstone, *Edward of Carnarvon, op. cit.* 83–7.
[2] *Guisborough,* 351–2; *Rishanger,* 213.
[3] *Rymer,* I, 952–4.

3 Caerlaverock Castle (Dunfriesshire)

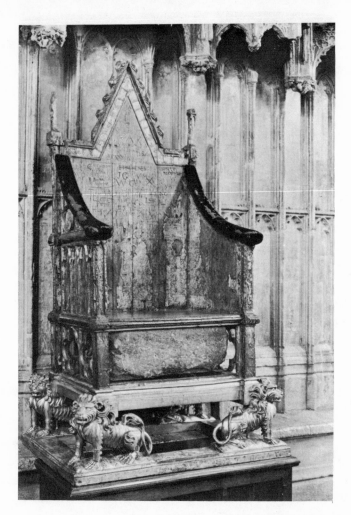

4 Coronation Chair with
the Stone of Destiny

5 The reputed effigy of Arnaud de Gabaston, father
of Peter of Gaveston, in Winchester Cathedral

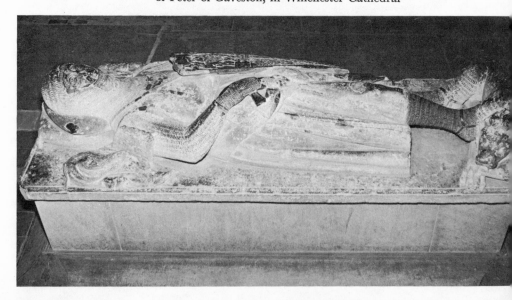

At the beginning of June, father and son began a *chevauchée* intended to avenge the defeat at Roslin, and to terrorize Scotland into grovelling submission. An impressive trek reached as far north as Kinloss Abbey on the Moray Firth, and thence by Strathspey into the heart of the Highlands at Boat of Garten and back through the Grampians to Kildrummy, Dundee, Scone, Dunblane, Cambuskenneth, and by November to winter quarters in Dunfermline.[1] The prince had his own headquarters set up at Perth, where he remained until March 1304. It had been a savage harrying of north-eastern Scotland, but it had its reward. An announcement of generous pardons for all Scots who surrendered to Edward's mercy (save five leaders, who of course included William Wallace) had been promulgated in January and had resulted in the surrender of Bruce, Comyn and many more, and the prince played a prominent part in the subsequent negotiations and receptions – amongst other Scottish leaders he entertained John Comyn. Reasonably generous surrender terms dated 9 February marked the end of another chapter in the sad story of Scottish rebellion.[2] Only one castle and one leader, apart from Wallace, still held out – the gallant young constable of Stirling Castle, Sir William Oliphant.[3] Oliphant, relying on the customary courtesies of chivalry, asked permission to send word to his leader Sir John de Soulis (now exiled in France) to inquire whether he might honourably surrender. Edward's answer was an unchivalrous refusal, and when the garrison at last surrendered, on 20 July, they were also refused the usual military honours and threatened with disembowelling and hanging. Perhaps Edward's fury was due to the fact that he had narrowly escaped death from a crossbow bolt shot from the walls.[4] In any event, it was a discreditable episode which met with some murmurs of disapproval, even from the English knights.

It was not until August 1304, that Edward was able to leave Scotland, and once again felt safe enough to order his

---

[1] E. M. Barron, *Scottish War, op cit.* 192–3, *Flores Hist.,* III, 113–4; H. Gough, *Itinerary of Edward I* (London, 1861), I, 279–83.

[2] *Rot. Parl.,* I, 212–13.

[3] *Flores Hist.,* III, 118, 'Miles satis magnanimus'; *Rishanger,* 223.

[4] *Trevet,* 403; *Rishanger,* 222–3.

exchequer back to Westminster from York, where it had been stationed for six-and-a-half years. He might feel that Scotland was at last subdued behind him, yet he knew that Wallace was still at large, and, what he did not know, Robert Bruce was plotting a second desertion in favour this time of his native land. The prince was now to fulfil another obligation contained in the Paris treaty – he was to do homage to the king of France on behalf of his father for his lands in Aquitaine. He was to be accompanied by an impressive company of notables, together with Florentine merchants to take care of the financial negotiations, and on 25 October he arrived at Dover ready to cross the Channel for Amiens where the homage ceremonies were planned for 1 November. Neither a promised French royal escort nor official safe-conducts had arrived by the agreed date. The prince with his father's full approval, therefore abandoned his journey.[1]

Edward, prince of Wales and earl of Chester, was now turned twenty. He was already experienced in affairs of state, he was toughened by campaigning against savage rebels in a cruel land, and he had earned the plaudits of the chroniclers and apparently the full confidence of his distinguished father. It was a short period of successful calm before an extraordinary and unexpected storm of great violence.

[1] C. Johnson, *The Homage for Guienne in 1304*, in *E.H.R.*, XXIII (1908), 728–9.

Chapter 4

DISCORD

Prince Edward spent most of the winter of 1304–5 at Langley, but he played a full part in the spring parliament which met at Westminster in March. There his new principate gave him added status and he 'and his council' heard petitions from the men of Wales separately.[1] While the parliament was in session, the prince lived at the royal palace at Kennington, and there was no sign of the astonishing upheaval which was about to occur.

On Monday, 14 June 1305, the king banished his son and heir from court, and ordered the Exchequer to refuse any requests from the prince for financial support until further notice. It was a totally unexpected explosion. The precise cause of the quarrel is not exactly known, but apparently the prince had incurred the king's wrath because he had insulted his chief minister Walter Langton, bishop of Coventry and Lichfield, treasurer of the Exchequer, and at that time the king's favourite minister. According to one chronicler, the prince had trespassed into a park belonging to Langton, and, on being accused of the fault, had roundly abused the bishop. Another version states that, aided and abetted by Peter of Gaveston, he had not only committed trespass but had also poached some of the bishop's deer. The king was determined to teach his son a drastic lesson in deportment. However, deprivation of financial support for nearly six months and expulsion from the court seems an unnecessarily severe sentence for what was certainly not a heinous offence. There is a reference to his disgrace in one of the prince's letters, which have survived from this period – he refers to 'certain words' which he had had with the bishop of Chester and which had been reported to the

[1] F. W. Maitland, *Memoranda de Parliamento 1305*, Rolls Series 1893.

41

king.[1] And later in this same year, when Sir William de Braose was imprisoned for 'contumelious words' to the royal judges, the sentence referred to the king's similar treatment of his own son.[2] But there may have been more cause for severity than is revealed in the records, and the suggestion that Gaveston was implicated could partly explain the affair.

The king was on his way to Chichester when the sentence was announced. There a special service was due to commemorate the translation of St Richard, which the king had himself witnessed nine years before. The prince therefore waited at Midhurst, next at Singleton in Sussex, and thence followed his father's progress along the south downs to Canterbury 'at a distance of ten or twelve leagues', hoping to be restored to favour. Without official help, the prince had to rely for supplies and sustenance on friends and relatives. His treasurer, Walter Reynolds, did his best, and his tutor Sir Guy Ferre, Sir Hugh Despenser (the elder), the earl of Lincoln, and Antony Bek bishop of Durham, are quoted in the prince's letters as his 'useful' friends, and even the king's almoner, Henry Blunsdon, contributed secretly. The prince's sister Joan, now countess of Gloucester, and his step-mother Queen Margaret also gave him sympathy and practical help. On 21 July it is recorded that he sent back with a gracious letter of thanks Joan's personal seal which she had lent to him – it was the equivalent of what a blank cheque could mean today. But, judging from his many letters at this time, the prince was never unduly embarrassed.[3] He busied himself with the affairs of his stud at Ditchling, and he continued to be active in soliciting favours for his friends, and especially for preferment for Walter Reynolds. By the end of July, the most severe restrictions began to be relaxed, and two of his personal yeomen were allowed to return to him. He also asked his stepmother to help in restoring to him the company of Gilbert

[1] *Ann. Lond.*, 138; H. Johnstone, *Letters*, 30. This remarkable series of some 800 letters written over a short period of five months is full of interest. Appendix IV below pp. 163–8. See also W. H. Blaaw in *Sussex Archaeological Collections*, II, 96–7.

[2] *Abbreviatio Placitorum* (Record Commission, 1811), 256–7; *Ann. Lond.*, 143.

[3] H. Johnstone, *Letters*, 34, 60, 61, 62, 67, 73, 102 and 133–4, and Appendix IV below.

de Clare and Peter of Gaveston, but with what result is not known.[1] He was next ordered to remain in or near Windsor Park until the opening of a parliament which was due at Westminster in September. He seems to have whiled away his time amusing himself with his greyhounds, and it was another month before his expulsion was at last rescinded. On 12 October 1305, a sumptuous banquet in the great hall of Westminster palace, at which the prince presided, marked the end of the royal estrangement.[2] The king could consider the episode closed; the prince was to remember both his friends and his enemies.[3]

It was during this period of royal discord that two significant events took place – the election of a new pope in June, and the execution of William Wallace in August. The new pope was Bertrand de Got, archbishop of Bordeaux, who was crowned as Pope Clement V. As a Gascon, his direct feudal lord was the king of England, and his background promised well for English interests. The king and his son were invited to the papal coronation which took place at Lyons in the following November, and, although neither accepted, a very powerful English delegation was sent with a magnificent present of gold plate from the king.[4] Pope Clement was not slow to respond to this friendly gesture – on 29 December 1305, he released the king from his oath to observe the charters,[5] on 1 January 1306 he granted father and son immunity from excommunication without the express order of the Holy See,[6] and, in response to the king's complaints against a very obstinate Archbishop Winchelsey of Canterbury, the pope summoned Winchelsey to Rome for a full investigation.[7] The English monarch could now feel certain that, when next he dealt with a rebellious Scotland, he was in no danger of a stab in the back from across the Channel – the new anglophile pope was soon to move both himself and his court to French Avignon.

[1] *Ibid.*, 70.
[2] *Ann. Lond.*, 143.
[3] See below pp. 52–3.
[4] *Flores Hist.*, III, 127.
[5] *Rymer*, I, 978.
[6] *Rymer*, I, 979.
[7] He was not to return to England until the new reign.

Since the great *chevauchée* of 1303–4, a crushed Scotland had not bothered England overmuch. The victorious Edward at his Lenten parliament of 1305 with unusual moderation had called upon three Scottish leaders – Robert Wishart, bishop of Glasgow, Robert Bruce, earl of Carrick and baron John de Moubray – to advise him on the future settlement of 'the kingdom' of Scotland.[1] As a result, a new 'constitution' was promulgated in September 1305 which partitioned Scotland into four judicial areas each governed jointly by an English and a Scottish judge, under the overall authority of the king's lieutenant in Scotland, who was to be the king's nephew John of Brittany, earl of Richmond. In spite of this façade of consultation and apparent regard for local participation, it is clear that Scotland was in fact once again a conquered country occupied by foreign garrisons, governed by foreign officials and at the mercy of a foreign king, and Edward's personal animosity was reserved for the man who had begun the Scottish revolt. William Wallace had at last been captured near Glasgow on 3 August by Sir John Menteith, keeper of Dumbarton castle, and, like Bruce, a deserter to Edward. Wallace was sent to London, and on 28 August he was given a formal trial in Westminster's palace hall by which a Scottish patriot was foredoomed to be convicted of 'treason' to a king of England. His execution as a traitor omitted no detail of the customary barbarities of the times. Wallace was dragged on a hurdle from Westminster to the Tower, thence to Aldgate and finally to Smithfield Elms where he was hanged, cut down while still alive, disembowelled and beheaded. His head was spiked on London Bridge, his heart and entrails burned to ashes, and his four quarters distributed to Newcastle, Berwick, Stirling and Perth.[2] It was the vengeance of King Edward of England which unwittingly helped to make William Wallace into an impeccable Scottish hero.

But Scotland was not as cowed as its English conquerors assumed. In the autumn of 1305, Robert Bruce had made a 'bond' with William Lamberton, bishop of St Andrews, for

[1] G. W. S. Barrow, *Bruce, op. cit.* 189 *et seq.*
[2] *Lanercost,* 176; J. Stevenson, *Documents Illustrative of Sir William Wallace, etc.* (Maitland Club, 1841), 187, 189, 193.

mutual aid in future perils, but this first indication of which way the wind was blowing had been kept secret.[1] Both Bruce and Wishart, bishop of Glasgow, had been in Scotland when Wallace had been captured and executed, and in the winter of 1305–6 there is no doubt that Robert Bruce was contemplating a final turning of his coat. On 10 February 1306, he was due to meet John the Red Comyn, lord of Badenoch (and recently one of the guardians of Scotland) for some kind of conspiratorial conference in the Greyfriars church at Dumfries. What exactly happened there will never now be known with certainty. The only undisputed fact is that the Comyn was murdered by the high altar, and that Robert Bruce, earl of Carrick, had to take responsibility for this sacrilegious deed.[2] Comyn had surrendered to Edward after the *chevauchée*, and it may be that he was reluctant to join with Bruce in another rising which could result in Bruce usurping the Scottish throne – after all, King 'Toom Tabard' was still alive, although in exile, and had a full-grown son and heir.

The news of Comyn's murder and Bruce's treachery spurred on King Edward to a last attempt at Scotland's overthrow, while in Scotland Bruce's fiery cross of revolt brought patriots flocking to his standard. On 25 March 1306, Bruce was crowned with a gold coronet as King Robert I of Scotland at Scone in spite of the fact that the Stone of Destiny was now at Westminster. On 27 March a second ceremony took place in order that the tradition that a Macduff must crown a Scottish king might be observed – Isabel of Fife, countess of Buchan, who was reputed to be Bruce's mistress, placed him on an improvised royal throne.[3] The English were faced yet again with a massive Scottish revolt.

But King Edward of England was not the man he had been – it was apparent that at last his giant's strength was ebbing, and that it would not be long before his son would have to take on the burdens of leadership. It was with this in mind, and perhaps

---

[1] See above p. 40, and F. Palgrave, *Docts and Recs illustrating the History of Scotland* (London, 1837) 323–4.

[2] *Guisborough*, 367; G. W. S. Barrow, *Bruce, op. cit.* 205–8.

[3] E. L. G. Stones, *Anglo Scottish Relations, 1174–1328* (Edinburgh, 1964), No. 35, 138; *Scalacronica*, 130, *Flores Hist.*, III, 129–30; *C.D.S.* II, no. 1914.

to signalize his renewed confidence in a prince who had acquitted himself well on more than one Scottish campaign, that on 22 May 1306, the king himself knighted his son in the chapel of the palace at Westminster, and he supported the new title with the grant of the duchy of Aquitaine, Oléron and the Agenais.[1] This was the major ceremony in what has been termed 'the largest mass knighting in medieval England'.[2] For nearly a century the authorities had been attempting to force those qualified to enter the order of knighthood and to accept its duties – without much success. This time almost three hundred candidates presented themselves, and one chronicler calculated that there were over a thousand knights present in London for the ceremonies.[3] It posed formidable problems of catering and lodging. The buildings of the Knights Templar on the Thames near the Lud Gate were requisitioned, and temporary tents and pavilions were erected in their gardens. The night of 21–22 May had to be spent in the prayer and meditation of the customary vigil, but it was in fact a night of chaos and wassail in the Temple. On the morrow, in the abbey at Westminster, Prince Edward knighted them all in a memorable ceremony which was followed by a banquet so splendid that it astounded the chroniclers. Over eighty minstrels played to the assembly, and a spate of oath-taking took place over a royal dish of swans. The king swore that, when Bruce was dealt with, he would once again make crusade, while his son swore never to sleep two nights in the same place until he reached Scotland.[4] The new position and standing of Prince Edward were now established beyond cavil – to Ponthieu and Montreuil, Wales and Chester had now been added the authority, wealth and prestige of Aquitaine. The old king was casting his mantle over the young prince who must soon succeed him.

The Scottish expedition of 1306 was carefully prepared and staged. In advance, Aymer de Valence, earl of Pembroke, was appointed the king's lieutenant on the eastern approaches

[1] *Rymer*, I, 983.

[2] *Flores Hist.*, III, 131; N. Denholm-Young in *History*, XXIX (1944), 107–19.

[3] *Ann. Lond.*, 146.

[4] *Langtoft*, 368.

while Henry Percy was appointed to a similar post on the western approaches. All forces were to concentrate at Carlisle on 8 July; the Cinque Ports' ships were to sail to Skinburness, the port of Carlisle; supplies of victuals were to be requisitioned from Ireland and Gascony as well as England, and the prince's forces included a useful contingent from Wales. On 8 June the prince left London for Scotland in advance of his father, who now found difficulty in riding. By 8 July, when the invasion was due to begin, the king had only reached Nottingham.

But, meanwhile, the news from beyond the Border was encouraging. De Valence on 26 June had routed Bruce in a fierce affray at Methven near Perth, and the newly crowned king of Scotland was retreating in disorder to the west.[1] At Dalry near Tyndrum he was again defeated by John Mac-dougal of Argyll, and his latest adventure seemed ignominiously at an end.[2] He dispatched his wife and the other ladies of his entourage in the care of one of his brothers, Sir Nigel Bruce, and the earl of Atholl to the greater safety of the castle of Kildrummy in the mountains of Aberdeenshire, while he himself dis-appeared into hiding.

The prince and Pembroke advanced north to besiege Kildrummy, where, after a Scottish traitor had set fire to the corn in the castle's hall, the garrison quickly surrendered.[3] The Scottish ladies escaped, but they were pursued and soon captured. There followed a reign of terror in which there is no doubt the prince was as ruthless and as vindictive as his father. The Scottish chronicler Barbour calls the prince 'a young bacheller, stark and fair', and goes on to term him 'the starkest man of ane'.[4] Their vengeance spared no one – the earl of Atholl, Sir Nigel Bruce, Simon Frazer of Oliver Castle and dozens of other Bruce supporters were hanged and executed, and Edward I's special malevolence was reserved for two of Bruce's ladies. Bruce's sister Mary and the countess of Buchan, who had crowned him, were placed in latticed turrets or cages of timber and iron on the walls of Roxburgh and Berwick

[1] *Guisborough*, 368; Barbour, *Bruce*, 27–31.
[2] Barbour, *Bruce*, 35ff; *Chron. Ford*, I, 342.
[3] Barbour, *Bruce*, 59–60.
[4] *Ibid.*, 71–6.

castles respectively. They were graciously granted the con-
venience of privies, but were otherwise exposed to the public
gaze, and suffered this cruel fate for over three years.[1] It is not
known where Bruce spent the ensuing months. It may have
been either in Norway or the Western Isles, or more probably
in the island of Rathlin, a few miles off the Antrim coast of
northern Ireland.

Campaigning north of the Border ceased as usual during the
winter. The prince went south while his father remained at
Lanercost Priory until he had to meet a parliament called to
Carlisle for January 1307. It was at this parliament that the
papal nuncio, the Spanish Cardinal Peter of Santa Sabina, was
persuaded to excommunicate Bruce and all who had shared in
the murder of Comyn, and yet another step forward was made
in the protracted negotiations which were to signalize peace
with France by the wedding of the prince and the French
princess.[2] The prince himself was deputed to lead an imposing
delegation to France in May which was to agree the final
arrangements.[3]

But on 26 February 1307, the old king had issued a very
significant ordinance at Lanercost. It ordered Peter of Gaveston
to leave England by the end of April and to stay away until
recalled, and both Peter and the prince were to take oaths upon
the Host that they would obey the royal ordinance faithfully.[4]
This was not a penal exile accompanied by public disgrace and
financial confiscations. Peter was treated generously – he was to
enjoy a pension of 100 marks a year while 'awaiting his recall',
and, depending on the results of an inquiry into his means and
property, this amount might be varied according to the king's
pleasure. There were neither official condemnations nor legal

---

[1] *Guisborough*, 367–9; *Flores Hist.*, III, 324; *Scalacronica*, 130; *Rishanger*,
229; G. W. S. Barrow, *Bruce, op. cit.* 228–30; F. Palgrave, *Documents, op.
cit.* 358–9.'A little house of timber in a tower, the sides latticed', says
the Scalacronica.

[2] *Lanercost*, 180. For the details of a curious suggestion that the prince
should marry a Spanish princess see H. Johnstone, *Edward of Carnarvon,
op. cit.* 120–1.

[3] *Rymer*, I, 1012.

[4] *Rymer*, I, 1010.

sanctions – it was simply stated that the expulsion was 'for certain reasons'.

What were these 'certain reasons'? All the chroniclers refer to this episode. Gaveston was 'charged with various misdemeanours'; the king 'fears that he loved his son inordinately'; the king saw that 'his son, the prince of Wales, had an inordinate affection for a certain Gascon knight'; Peter was banished 'on account of the undue intimacy which the young Lord Edward had adopted towards him, publicly calling him his brother'; the prince 'chose and was determined to tie an unbreakable bond of affection with him above all mortals'.[1] But one chronicler – Guisborough – was more specific. He gives an account of an actual quarrel between father and son over the Gascon favourite. According to this version, the prince approached the king through Langton to ask that Gaveston might be made count of Ponthieu – Montreuil in his stead. The king was outraged, and in a fury sent for his son. 'You baseborn whoreson,' he shouted, 'do you want to give away lands now, you who never gained any. As the Lord lives, if it were not for fear of breaking up the kingdom you should never enjoy your inheritance.' He seized the prince by the hair, tore out as much as he could, and then drove him out. One other chronicler refers to the same incident but maintains that it was the earldom of Cornwall which was asked for Gaveston, and that in reply the king knocked the prince down and kicked him.[2] The king could find no fault with Gaveston's public service[3] but he was obviously alarmed at his private relationships with the prince. The evidence strongly suggests that he suspected a homosexual infatuation which he was determined to thwart if he could.

For the moment, the prince and Peter obeyed the king's command. The prince, however, made it clear that his affection

[1] *Trevet*, 411; *Scalacronica*, 139; *Ann. Paul*, 255; *Lanercost*, 184; G. L. Haskins, *A chronicle of the civil wars of Edward II* (the 'Cleopatra' chronicle) in *Speculum*, XIV (1939), 73–81.

[2] *Guisborough*, 382–3; *Speculum ut sup.* 75.

[3] For the story of Gaveston's alleged 'desertion,' together with about twenty more of the younger baronage, see H. Johnstone, *Edward of Carnarvon*, *op. cit.* 115–17. 'Truancy' rather than 'desertion' would be a fairer description – and he was in good company.

for Peter was unabated – he accompanied him to the coast, bought him costly tunics 'after the Gascon fashion', presented him with valuable tapestries and two quilts, and liberally rewarded his entourage with ready money. And, by the prince's express command, Peter was told to make for Crécy in Ponthieu and not for Gascony. The exile was seen off by the prince from Dover early in May.[1]

After a short stay at Langley, the disconsolate prince prepared to go north again to rejoin the Scottish war. Bruce had been strong enough to return, and had landed in Kintyre and proceeded to Turnberry on the Ayrshire coast with new reinforcements, while his brothers, Thomas and Alexander,[2] sailed direct to the coast of Galloway. Both Bruce's brothers were soon captured and both were executed as Wallace had been, in spite of the fact that Alexander was in holy orders, but Bruce himself had enjoyed a modest prelude of success near Turnberry, and on 10 May he had defeated Aymer de Valence at the battle of Loudoun Hill a few miles east of Kilmarnock. Three days later, he was able to pursue Ralph de Monthermer into the shelter of Ayr's castle walls.[3] Bruce's star was in the ascendant.

By 16 June the prince had reached Northampton from where he dutifully sent his father a present of two barrels of sturgeon. Ten days later, he reached Carlisle. On 3 July the old king – he was now desperately ill – attempted to ride to the Border. On two successive days he managed two miles. After a day's rest he heroically went on again, and by 6 July he had reached Burgh-by-Sands near the ford over the Solway Firth at Sandy-wath. On the morning of 7 July 1307, as his servants lifted him from his bed to take food, he fell back dead.[4] The old 'Hammer of the Scots' had not even been able to reach the Border.

[1] *Additional M.S.S.*, British Museum, 22923 f6.

[2] *Lanercost*, 179–80, Alexander had had a brilliant career at Cambridge University, and had been granted a living near Wigtown and subsequently made dean of Glasgow. See *The Story of England by Robert Manning of Brunne*, ed. F. J. Furnivall, Rolls Series, I, 12–13.

[3] *C. Oman, op. cit.* II, 83–4; Barbour, *Bruce*, 129, 136–42; *Guisborough*, 378.

[4] *Guisborough*, 377–9; *Trevet*, 412–13.

Chapter 5

CORONATION
AND
MARRIAGE

A far-famed and formidable king of nearly sixty-eight – a very great age in those days – was now succeeded *par descente de héritage*, and with no dispute, by a son of twenty-three.[1] King Edward II's official regnal years date from the day of his father's death, although it was nearly eight months before he was actually crowned.

What did the new king inherit? He was now head of a kingdom whose exchequer was heavily in debt, whose man-power and resources had been strained by warfare in Wales, Flanders, Gascony and Scotland, and whose revenues were in pawn to the Frescobaldi and the Bardi, hated moneylenders of Florence. The English baronage held to a tradition of oligarchic privilege which had several times in the previous hundred years humbled the monarchy, and which, in spite of what later hindsight has discerned, paid little heed to new political forces emerging from below. At the very moment of accession, yet another Scottish expedition was in preparation – this time to face the full-scale rebellion of the usurper Robert Bruce. It was not a very happy heritage.

But the new king had assets. He was physically strong and more than usually handsome. He had already had experience of four campaigns in the difficult terrain of Scotland in which he had acquitted himself well. He had had the training and advice of excellent tutors, and an early pre-view of state affairs as prince-regent. He had displayed a creditable interest in the

[1] *Rymer*, II, 1.

51

arts, music and architecture, although his addiction to humble crafts and rural sports was more unorthodox and less respected. His scholarship may have been questionable, but medieval barons would not have held that against him. His regard for the Church was sincere to the point of enthusiasm. He was endowed with a pleasant personality which endeared him to high and low even though the Plantagenet temper had brought him into conflict with his father. After the abnormally long reign of Edward I and all the civil strife and disappointments of its final years, there was a general mood of happy expectancy to make the path of the new king smoother. 'God had endowed him with every gift and had made him equal to or indeed more excellent than other kings' says his contemporary biographer, and his accession was greeted 'with exceptional rejoicing' says another. But the rejoicings were not to last long, and one chronicler was gloomy enough to refer to the new king as a Rehaboam succeeding a Solomon.[1]

It took Edward nearly a fortnight to reach his father's bier, and it was not until the beginning of September that he was ready to leave the Border. Meanwhile, the old king's corpse had been escorted to Waltham Abbey with all due solemnity, and immediate ceremonies of homage had been staged at Carlisle for the available English baronage and at Dumfries for such Scottish baronage as had not yet joined Bruce. Now Edward II lost no time in making it quite clear that a new reign had begun.

Antony Bek, bishop of Durham and titular Patriarch of Jerusalem,[2] who had quarrelled with Edward I but who had been a steady friend to the prince, was immediately restored to his palatinate and given the honour of guarding the royal corpse. Walter Langton, bishop of Lichfield and Treasurer, was forthwith stripped of office and possessions and imprisoned in the Tower – it was the heavy price he had to pay for having

[1] *Flores Hist.*, III, 137; *Vita*, 40; *Trevisa*, 299; *Lanercost*, 183. 'One of the strongest men of his realm', says *Scalacronica*, 136.

[2] C. M. Fraser, *A History of Antony Bek 1283–1311* (London, 1957), *passim*. The Caerlaverock chronicler, 22–3 calls him 'le plus vaillant clerk du royaume', and Edward as prince had referred to him as 'our entire and certain friend'; H. Johnstone, *Letters*, 62.

resented the strong language of a young prince. The congenial Walter Reynolds was made Treasurer in his place. Robert Winchelsey, archbishop of Canterbury who had defied Edward I and was still abroad, was recalled; only illness prevented his prompt return to royal favour. On the other hand, William Melton, the new keeper of the privy seal, John Langton, bishop of Chichester, the new chancellor, and John Benstead, the new keeper of the wardrobe, were all tried and trusted servants of the old king. The act which clearly showed which way the wind of change was now blowing was the immediate recall of Peter of Gaveston from his exile in Ponthieu.

As early as 6 August 1307, Edward II, by a charter sealed in the presence of seven earls and other magnates, went even further – his recalled 'brother Perrot' was ennobled. To the consternation of most of the baronage, the obscure Gascon knight was made earl of Cornwall and granted all the manors, castles and properties appertaining to that rich royal appanage.[1] Furthermore, he was affianced to the king's niece Margaret of Clare, daughter of his favourite sister Joan of Acre and sister to Gilbert de Clare, now earl of Gloucester, who had been a favourite companion of the king's youth. There were rumours too, that the king had supported the new earl of Cornwall by endowing him with the considerable treasure which Walter Langton had accumulated at the Temple.[2] Old Henry de Lacy, earl of Lincoln, was one of the few who approved of this spectacular promotion, but in general Edward II had begun his reign with a prodigious shock to the contemporary establishment.

As the winter was coming on, it was with his peers' agreement that the Scottish expedition was abandoned. The king had wisely left behind him John of Brittany, earl of Richmond, and Aymer de Valence, earl of Pembroke, to look after affairs on the Border, while he himself had moved south to meet his first parliament which had been summoned to Northampton for October.[3] It had to provide for the normal expenses of the

[1] *Rymer*, II, 2.
[2] *Ann. Paul.*, 257; *Murimuth*, 9–10.
[3] *Rymer*, II, 16, 84, 114.

crown and for three abnormally expensive royal occasions – the funeral of the late king, and the marriage and the coronation of the new; and it promptly did its duty. The normal proceedings of this parliament were interrupted for a week while the royal obsequies took place. The corpse of Edward Longshanks was nobly escorted from Waltham Abbey, where it had lain by Harold's grave for nearly four months, and on 27 October it was at last interred between the tombs of Henry III and Edmund Crouchback in the abbey at Westminster. The casket was a simple box of black Purbeck marble. Its famous inscription *'Edvardus Primus Scotorum malleus hic est, 1308. Pactum Serva'* was added (with its wrong date) in the sixteenth century. The tomb of the greatest of the Plantagenets can still be seen, but it is without its gilding and without the elaborate and massive carved wooden canopy which originally surmounted it, and which were lost in the sacrilegious riots which accompanied the funeral of Pulteney, earl of Bath, in 1764. Dean Stanley, historian of the Abbey, suggested that the tomb was left in its comparatively simple state in order that, when appropriate, the pact reputedly enjoined upon his son by the dying king (and referred to in the later inscription) might be honoured, and his bones carried at the head of an English army conquering Scotland, while his heart struck fear into the infidel in the Holy Land. In fact, it was decreed that every two years after the funeral the tomb was to be opened, the wax of the cerecloth renewed and the tomb resealed until the hour of victory over Scotland, and therefore for a new crusade, had struck. This strange ceremony was regularly carried out until the fall of the dynasty, when the last Plantagenet was deposed by the Lancastrian usurper. The theory that the present plainness of the tomb of Edward I betrays the deliberate slight of an unfilial son is untenable.[1]

Two days after the royal funeral, Peter of Gaveston was married in a magnificent ceremony at Berkhamsted to Margaret de Clare, and Edward's biographer expatiates on the Gascon's unpopularity. 'The magnates of the land hated him because he alone found favour in the king's eyes and lorded it over them

[1] A. P. Stanley, *Historical Memorials of Westminster Abbey* (London, 1882), 128–30.

6 Scarborough Castle

7 Bruce v. de Bohun at Bannockburn

quasi secundus rex' . . . the more the king was told to damp his ardour 'the greater grew his love and tenderness towards Piers'.[1] On 2 December 1307, Gaveston promoted a grand tournament at Wallingford (which had come to him as earl of Cornwall) to celebrate his marriage.[2] In the lists, the younger and more athletic knights of Gaveston's side were much too good for the earls of Hereford, Arundel and Surrey and the older barons, and this added to their resentment of the foreign favourite. But, says the chronicler, the king had an 'unswerving affection' for him, and by public decree 'Sir Piers Gaveston' was in future to be called only by his new title 'Earl of Cornwall'.[3]

Edward was happy to be able to spend his first Christmas as king in the company of 'brother Perrot'. In the New Year, he left England for France and his own marriage, and he left behind him the earl of Cornwall as his regent.[4] It was yet another and an even more spectacular insult to the older baronage of England.

On 25 January 1308, Edward's marriage to the princess Isabella took place in the church of Notre Dame at Boulogne in the presence of a very distinguished company, which included the bride's father, Philip IV of France, and a great assembly of the nobles of both countries. The bridegroom was twenty-three and his bride sixteen years old. On the day before the ceremony, Edward paid homage to Philip for the territories of Aquitaine and Ponthieu, and, on returning to Dover, immediate preparations were made for a very much overdue coronation.[5]

The coronation of Edward II in 1308 has given subsequent historians ample excuse for much learned and sometimes acrimonious debate. The ceremony was postponed for a week, and one chronicler alleges that this was because the baronage refused to attend unless Gaveston were banished, while another says that it was on account of the baron's objections to Gaveston carrying the royal crown. The more likely reason was that the

[1] *Vita*, 1–2.
[2] Apparently two other celebration tournaments were held, see *Ann. Paul.*, 259.
[3] *Vita*, 3.
[4] *Rymer*, II, 28; 'Mira res' says *Vita*, 3.
[5] *Walsingham*, I, 121; *Trokelowe*, 65.

king was hoping that Archbishop Winchelsey could arrive back in time to preside. Unfortunately, the archbishop was still too ill to travel, and the ceremony had to be performed by Henry Woodlock, bishop of Winchester. Another controversy relates to the language of the royal oath. The king spoke in French and not in Latin, and this fact has been adduced to prove that Edward was illiterate.[1] It is now believed that he spoke in French simply because he wished his audience to understand what he was saying – for Edward, and for most of those in the Abbey, French was their mother tongue. A third and much more serious debate concerns the fourth clause of the royal oath, that the king would 'uphold and defend the laws and the righteous customs which the community of your realm shall determine'. The exact interpretation of this pledge led to much argument in Edward's reign and has filled many pages of learned journals in our own times. The lawyers of 1308 had seen Edward's father make light of oaths, but it had for long been an axiom that even the king was subject to the law, and it was accepted that ancient customs were as binding as new enactments. It was the phrase 'which the community of your realm shall determine' which caused most of the argument.[2] Who constituted the 'community'? And how was it to choose or decide? These were difficult problems which caused immediate trouble, and remained unsolved for centuries.

The coronation ceremony was attended not only by the baronage but also by 'suitable' representatives of the cities,

---

[1] *Ann. Paul.*, 260, see below pp. 152–3 and Appendix I, p. 157.

[2] H. G. Richardson and G. O. Sayles, *Early Coronation Records*, Bulletin of the Inst. of Historical Research, XIII, 140; H. G. Richardson in *T.R.H.S.* (4th series), XXIII (1941), 135 and 144–5. For the word 'communalte' see M. V. Clarke, *Medieval Representation and Consent* (Oxford, 1936), 171–2. The French has 'aura eslu', and the Latin elegerit'. cf. Appendix I below, p. 157. For B. Wilkinson's views, see *Historical Essays in honour of James Tait*, Manchester 1933, 405–16; *Speculum*, XIX (1944), 445–69; *E.H.R.*, LXX (1955), 581–600, and his *Constitutional History of Mediaeval England* (London, 1952), II, 85–111. For H. G. Richardson's views, see *T.R.H.S.*, 4th series, XXIII (1941), 135–58; *Speculum*, XIX (1944), 445–69; XXIII (1948), 630–40; XXIV (1949), 44–75. For R. S. Hoyt's views, see *Traditio* XI (1955), 235–57; *E.H.R.*, LXXI (1956), 353–83.

boroughs and shires, and it was both elaborate and spectacular. To the general indignation, the crown and the sword of St Edward were carried before the king in the procession by the earl of Cornwall. And a normally joyful occasion – one chronicler states that the Londoners fancied they were seeing the New Jerusalem – was marred by the collapse of a wall which killed one of the attendant knights, and by the fact that at the coronation banquet the earl of Cornwall had the effrontery to wear royal purple instead of cloth of gold. Furthermore, the service at the banquet was apparently not all it ought to have been.[1] The lavish ceremonies could not disguise the fact that the 'community of the realm' was face to face with the problem of the king's wanton affection for and extravagant patronage of Peter of Gaveston.

There is no evidence that Gaveston was either incompetent or lacking in courage, but there is ample evidence to show that Edward's favour was over-generous and Gaveston's reactions tactless beyond measure. The earldom of Cornwall was a part of the royal estate which ought not to have been in the hands of a foreigner. The niece of the monarch was too high-born a lady to be given in marriage to 'a mere roturier'.[2] Some distinguished French visitors to the coronation observed that Edward preferred the couch of Peter to that of his queen, and all men resented the fact that there were now two kings in England, one in name and the other in effect. There was general detestation of the king's worship of his 'idol', and it was indecent that the king should give away his own wedding presents to his minion.[3] The baronage of England, moreover, did not take kindly to a royal favourite who could unhorse them in the lists, and who could also pierce the armour of their dignity with his barbed Gascon wit. It is difficult today to understand why the tough barons of fourteenth-century England were so incensed at the nicknames invented for them, and it is equally difficult to appreciate the Gascon's wit. Thomas of Lancaster was 'a

---

[1] *Ann. Paul.*, 259–62 an eyewitness account; *Bridlington*, 32; *Walsingham*, I, 121–2.

[2] The phrase is Sir James Ramsay's in *Genesis*, I, 3, but it is inaccurate, see *supra* p. 30.

[3] *Ann. Paul.*, 258, 259, 262.

fiddler', Pembroke was 'Joseph the Jew', Gloucester was a 'cuckold's bird', Warwick was the 'black hound of Arden' – here are picturesque epithets but no obvious brilliance.[1]

The barons seem to have bound themselves by some kind of mutual oath to obtain the early and total banishment of the royal favourite. In April, in the so-called 'Declaration of 1308',[2] the earls quoted the controversial clause of the new coronation oath to reinforce their united demand that Gaston should be exiled – the king, they said, was bound by his oath to obey their decision. Another clause in the Declaration first announced what constitutional lawyers have since termed the 'doctrine of capacities' – it declared that homage was not due to the king in person but only to the crown as an institution.[3] That this was a questionable argument is proved by the fact that the barons themselves were to quote it later as part of an indictment against one of their own number, the younger Despenser, who had invented it, and it was not repeated during the various 'constitutional' crises of the following years. But it was clear that the new king was now face to face with a formidable revolt of most of his baronage. Even the old and powerful earl of Lincoln, who had at first supported Edward, now joined his critics, and only Sir Hugh Despenser, the elder, remained his avowed supporter, while Richmond and Gloucester refused to commit themselves to either side. At the council which met at Westminster on 28 April 1308, the barons were sufficiently bold to appear fully armed 'in self defence' and 'because they feared treachery'.[4] They demanded the immediate dismissal of Gaveston. Civil war seemed inevitable.

But at this point the king wisely gave way. On 18 May 1308, his letters patent granted all that the barons had demanded.[5] Gaveston was to be stripped of his titles and to quit the realm by 25 June, and Archbishop Winchelsey, who had at last arrived home, declared that, if Gaveston failed to obey the

[1] *Brut*, I, 206–7; *Walsingham*, I, 115; J. Harvey, *The Plantagenets* (London, 1963), 78.

[2] *Vita*, 4.

[3] *Ann. Lond.*, 153–4; *Bridlington*, 33; E. Salisbury in *E.H.R.*, XXXIII (1917), 78. For the 'doctrine of capacities' see *Maddicott*, 81–2.

[4] *Ann. Paul.*, 213; *Vita*, 5.

[5] *Rymer*, II, 44–5 and 48–51.

sentence or attempted to return, he would be excommunicated. But Edward ensured that his friend's exile would not be too irksome. English manors and castles to the value of £2,000 were granted to him, and similar properties of similar value in Aquitaine, and on 16 June he was appointed the king's lieutenant in Ireland. One chronicler asserts that, in addition, Gaveston was supplied with blank royal charters which he could use as he wished.[1] Gaveston and his lavish household set sail for Ireland by the date stipulated, and the king gave him a significant royal send-off from Bristol's crowded quays.

If the first twelve months of the reign of Edward II had begun in optimistic rejoicing, they had ended in sordid strife. Civil war had only just been averted by the king's surrender – the further outlook was gloomy.

[1] *Lanercost*, 187.

Chapter 6

THE ORDINANCES
AND
GAVESTON

While royal favouritism and baronial jealousy preoccupied England, Robert Bruce was free to consolidate rebellion in Scotland. It involved a bitter civil war north of the Border. After a clash near Inverurie in Aberdeenshire, where he defeated John Comyn, earl of Buchan and nephew of the exiled 'Toom Tabard',[1] Bruce set about teaching all his opponents a drastic lesson. The brutal harrying of Buchan was as savage an example of 'scorched earth' policy as William the Norman's harrying of the rebellious north of England in 1069. 'For fifty years,' wrote the Aberdonian Barbour, 'Men remembered the herschip of Buchan.'[2] Bruce's march to supreme authority in Scotland was over the corpses of many Scots and over many devastated Scottish acres – it is as well for his subsequent reputation that the treacheries and savageries of his early career have mercifully been overlooked in the light of his later heroisms. And while Robert Bruce was conquering the north, his only surviving brother Edward was occupied in as devastating an overrunning of Galloway and the south-west. The English could only cling to such major strongholds as Perth, Stirling, Bothwell, Edinburgh, Roxburgh and Berwick in the east and south, while their urgent calls for help from a harassed Edward II at Westminster had to go unanswered.[3]

An international complication now added further to Edward's

[1] Barbour, *Bruce*, 155.
[2] *Ibid.*, 156.
[3] *C.D.S.*, III, No. 80, IV, No. 1837.

difficulties. His father-in-law Philip IV of France, in desperate need of funds and having exhausted, and therefore having expelled, his Jewish financiers, had recently been turning greedy eyes on the wealth of the Order of the Knights Templars. Originally founded as a secret religious military order to defend the Holy Places against the infidel, the Templars had spread to most European countries and had accumulated enormous treasure and properties. They were now, in addition, international bankers as successful as the Italians, and their Temple in Paris was the centre of the thirteenth-century European money market. In England, too, they were rich and firmly established in the London Temple where their own wealth and the wealth of others were stored under guard, and where they were permitted to live a separate and priviliged life by the Thames between the cities of London and Westminster.

On 13 October 1307, Philip IV had suppressed the French Templars on grounds of alleged heresy and indecent secret rituals. Torture of the foulest kind extracted many confessions, and burning at the stake was the punishment meted out to many probably innocent victims. The Templars' treasure and properties were seized to help royal finances, and Philip went even further – he used his influence over the new Gascon pope, Clement V, to urge his fellow monarchs to follow his example. Edward II had the English church solidly behind him in resisting such orders from foreign powers, and in rejecting alien methods of torture to ensure confessions. But the temptation of obtaining welcome financial loot in good company was much too strong to be resisted for long. On 10 January 1308, the Order was also suppressed in England, Scotland and Ireland, in spite of an almost total lack of reliable evidence to support the gross charges of Philip IV and the papal inquisitors. The Knights of St John of Jerusalem were officially intended to be the ultimate beneficiaries, but, in the meantime, Edward was not the only monarch whose private funds benefited from so rich a windfall, and his young queen's dowry had come from the confiscated funds of the French Templars. Nevertheless, it is to the credit of England's ruling caste that, although not usually averse to severity, they refused to sanction torture or the stake and Edward's reluctance in this tragic affair contrasts favourably with the shameless enthusiasm of his father-in-law.[1]

But Edward II was now less worried by trials of Templars and by rebellion in Scotland than by the banishment of his beloved Gaveston. His not unskilful machinations to ensure a speedy return had begun the moment Gaveston left England. Thomas, earl of Lancaster, was the most powerful of the younger barons, and on 9 May 1308 Edward confirmed his inheritance of the stewardship of England in an attempt to win his favour.[2] Archbishop Winchelsey was engaged in certain disputes with the Frescobaldi concerning coining rights – Edward ordered the Italians to give way in a move to appease the obstinate old prelate.[3] Henry Percy, another of the younger barons, was favoured by the gift of Scarborough Castle as his northern residence. And in August, at a council of the baronage held at Northampton, Edward went so far in placating opposition that he dismissed Sir Hugh Despenser (the elder), who had been one of his father's companions in arms, and who was his own most loyal supporter, and also deprived Nicholas de Segrave of his post as marshal – they had both shown favour to Gaveston.[4] Edward's biographer writes that Edward 'bent one after another to his will with gifts, promises and blandishments', and that the only baron to withstand him was the earl of Warwick – Gaveston's 'black hound of Arden'.[5] In addition, Edward wrote to the pope asking that Winchelsey's conditional excommunication of Gaveston should be annulled, and pleased his father-in-law by granting Ponthieu and Montreuil to his young bride Isabella.[6] He carefully looked after Gaveston's English properties, and added to his possessions in Gascony with the connivance of

[1] *Guisborough*, 392; C. G. Addison, *The Knights Templars* 3rd ed. (London 1854); C. Perkins in *A.H.R.*, XV (1910), 252–63 and in *E.H.R.*, XXIV, 432–7, XXV, 209–230; Tout, *Chapters*, II, 315, 324, 338; Tout, *Place*, 207; A. M. Sandys in *Essays presented to T. F. Tout* (Manchester, 1925), 147–62. The Order was finally suppressed on 26 May 1312 at the Council of Vienne.

[2] *Rymer*, II, 44.

[3] *Rymer*, II, 45.

[4] *Ann. Paul.*, 264.

[5] *Vita*, 6.

[6] *Rymer*, II, 49–50.

Gloucester and Percy. Meanwhile, Gaveston himself was proving an excellent lieutenant in Ireland. His generosity was remarked upon favourably, his civilizing influence on the uncouth local manners was successful – it is recorded that in a rude age he was the rare owner of three silver forks 'for eating pears'. He dealt efficiently with rebellion in Munster and Thomond.[1]

The king's appeasement policy was, however, of no ultimate avail in the face of a general revolt of the baronage, which derived not only from their hatred of the foreign favourite but also from the old grievances which had led them to enforce the Confirmation of the Charters. In February 1309 the barons' plans for reform were concerted, and, when a full parliament met at Westminster on 27 April, the king was presented with a long schedule of familiar baronial demands – royal purveyance had become intolerable, royal officials were exceeding their authority, the coinage was debased, justice was too long delayed, and the royal household was extravagant and in need of reform and new personnel.[2] Edward proposed that, in return for his agreement to reforms, Gaveston should be recalled and restored to his title and estates. The barons refused, and the session was adjourned to a further meeting at Stamford which was called for July.

Before the Stamford meeting took place, the king's diplomacy had achieved better success. The pope had finally agreed to rescind Winchelsey's threats of excommunication, and the earls of Lincoln, Pembroke and Surrey were now persuaded to desert their peers and support the king. Only Winchelsey and Warwick remained irreconcilable.[3] Edward therefore acted swiftly. Gaveston was recalled, and Edward met him at Chester. They boldly appeared side by side at the Stamford parliament, where Edward was prepared to make concessions as the price of approval for Gaveston's return and for the restoration of his

[1] *Murimuth*, 11, 12; *Ann. Lond.*, 156; J. Conway Davies, *The Baronial opposition to Edward II* (London, 1967), 86 and 107–10; the reference to forks is from *Sussex Archaeological Collections*, VII, 204n.

[2] *Rot. Parl.*, I, 443–5. For the baronial tournament at Dunstable, which preceded the parliament, see *Maddicott*, 95–102.

[3] *Vita*, 6–7.

title and properties. The so-called Statute of Stamford accepted all eleven articles submitted by the barons on behalf of the 'Communalté'. They were for the most part a repetition of the *Articuli super Cartas* of 1300 – purveyance would be limited, the royal household would be purged, and Gaveston's return was approved. The *quid pro quo* of Stamford was one of Edward's few constitutional victories.

But if Edward was temporarily delighted, the folly of Gaveston soon wrecked his hopes of permanent success. It was now that the continued *turpia cognomina* of the Gascon's forked tongue roused the baronage to fury, and his high-handed treatment of a member of the earl of Lancaster's household foolishly lost Edward that earl's valuable support.[1] At a council of his barons, which the king summoned to York in October, five of the earls, including Lancaster, refused to appear, and in December action had to be taken against 'scandalmongers' and baronial armed gatherings.[2] But over Christmas 1309 the king and his 'brother Perrot' were again able to pass pleasant days together at Langley in 'long-wished-for sessions of daily and intimate conversation'.[3]

In February 1310, a parliament was due at Westminster. Once again the five unreconciled earls – Lancaster, Hereford, Warwick, Oxford and Arundel – stayed away 'because of Peter'. The king, supported only by Gloucester, Richmond and Surrey, dispatched Gaveston to the north for his greater safety, and in order that the earls might be persuaded to attend a parliament and provide urgently needed funds. The earls did attend, but, openly defiant, they appeared fully armed with their military retainers, and, in conjunction with Archbishop Winchelsey and the bishops, immediately presented to the king yet another statement of grievances. They demanded that a reform commission should be given powers to take all necessary action, and Edward saw no alternative to submission.[4] On 16 March 1310, a committee known as the Lords Ordainers was

---

[1] *Flores Hist.*, III, 152; Tout, *Place*, 12–13; J. Conway Davies, *op. cit.* 82–5.
[2] *Guisborough*, 384.
[3] *Vita*, 8.
[4] *Ann. Lond.*, 168–9.

set up by letters patent to reform the royal government and the royal household. A glossing chronicler could quote the ancient legal maxim that 'what touches all must be approved by all' but no commoners found places in this oligarchical conclave.[1] Twenty-one Ordainers were chosen in the Painted Chamber at Westminster by a complicated system of indirect election and co-option. The bishops elected two earls, the earls elected two bishops, and these four then elected two barons. The resulting six then co-opted fifteen others, and in the end the Ordainers included Archbishop Winchelsey, six bishops, eight earls – omitting only Surrey and Oxford who were not present and, of course, Gaveston of Cornwall – and six lesser barons. It was far from being democratic but it was not wholly unrepresentative – the bishop of Chichester was friendly to the king as were the earls of Richmond and Gloucester, and Robert Clifford and William Marshall among the barons were both Edward's men.

The commission issued six Ordinances forthwith, but its main document was not ready until August 1311. Until that date the king had over a year in which he might be able once again to circumvent his critics. On 30 April 1310, Langton, bishop of Chichester and chancellor, was ordered to attend upon the king at Windsor and to accompany him wherever he went, taking the great seal and the justices of the king's bench with him. Langton refused, and was promptly replaced by Walter Reynolds, the king's old friend and tutor.[2] In June, Surrey was bribed by gifts of castles and land in the Peak district, and Richmond was given valuable fairs and markets, while lavish grants to Gaveston continued.[3]

In September, Edward in desperation attempted to stage a diversion – he summoned his baronage to an expedition against the Scots. Gaveston, summoned as earl of Cornwall, of course obeyed, but the only other earls to join him were Gloucester and Surrey. In defiance of the Ordainers, Edward appointed one of his friends, John de Segrave, brother of the dismissed marshal, warden of Scotland, and he himself, with an ill-disciplined army which included a wild contingent from Wales, marched north,

[1] *Rymer*, II, 105.
[2] *Ann. Paul.*, 269.
[3] *Rymer*, II, 108.

leaving the earl of Lincoln as keeper of the realm behind him. By October, Edward had reached Linlithgow, and he remained on the Border until the following July (1311). Bruce and his supporters avoided all direct action, but Gaveston was able to take an army as far as Perth, and successfully harried the country between there and the Grampians. Gloucester acted similarly in Ettrick, while Edward remained in overall command at Berwick. As a military operation it was neither a spectacular success nor a dismal failure, but as a political manoeuvre it certainly failed – the Ordainers were not to be so easily diverted.

Early in the year 1311, Edward lost two valued supporters – Henry de Lacy, earl of Lincoln and Edward's regent, died in February, and Antony Bek, bishop of Durham, died in March. Both had been the experienced ministers of his father, and both had become a balancing force against extreme measures – they were a sad loss both to the barons and to Edward. Gloucester was appointed regent in Lincoln's place, but one baron especially benefited from Lincoln's death – Thomas, earl of Lancaster. Thomas was of the blood royal – his father was Edmund Crouchback, Edward's crusading uncle, and his sister was the queen of France. From Edmund he had inherited the earldoms of Lancaster, Leicester and Derby, and now by right of his wife, who was the sole heiress of Lincoln, he added the earldoms of Lincoln and Salisbury to already vast estates. 'I do not believe,' wrote Edward's biographer, 'that any duke or count under the Roman empire received as much from the profits of his lands as Thomas, earl of Lancaster.'[1] He was about seven years older than the king, and by virtue of his rank, his wealth, and his private army he at once took over the leadership of the baronial discontent. He was of course an implacable enemy to Gaveston.

Earl Thomas's first duty on the death of his father-in-law Lincoln was to render homage for his two new earldoms, and he rode north to find the king. Edward was at Berwick, and therefore technically at that time in Scotland. The earl, ever ready for a quarrel, maintained that he must pay fealty within the

[1] *Vita*, 29. J. Conway Davies, *op. cit.*, 107–10; *Maddicott*, 115. For Lancaster's wealth see Tout *Chapters*, II, 184–5 and *Maddicott*, 8–66.

English realm, and therefore that the king should cross the Tweed to meet him. Edward finally agreed, and the ceremony of homage was performed at Haggerston just south of the Border. But it was noted that at the ceremony the earl refused to salute the earl of Cornwall, and Edward readily took the hint. Gaveston was sent to the comparative safety of Bamburgh Castle while the king travelled south to meet his barons in a parliament at Westminster (to which the commons were also summoned) in order that the Ordinances prepared by the Lords Ordainers could be approved and officially promulgated.

The Ordinances of 1311 were set out in forty-one articles – including the original six. Edward arrived late from a pilgrimage to Canterbury, which may have been a feeble attempt at last-minute delay, and, having read through the complete list of Ordinances, he once more attempted to strike a bargain. If the barons would leave Gaveston in possession of his titles and estates, Edward would accept any of the Ordinances which referred to himself and his own rights and duties. But the barons were not to be bargained with – they were fully prepared for civil war unless the king accepted the Ordinances *in toto*. The king's advisers counselled acceptance, and, on 27 September 1311, the Ordinances were publicly read at Paul's Cross in the presence of their authors, and on 11 October they received the royal seal of assent.[1]

Edward's biographer gives a very clear and contemporary account of these proceedings, and it is significant that he prefaced it with a lengthy dissertation on the follies and pride of Gaveston, and that he reproduced in full only one clause of the Ordinances – the twentieth, which referred to Gaveston's exile.[2] The Lords Ordainers were a committee of the baronage whose objectives were, first, to obtain the perpetual banishment of Gaveston and other royal favourites, and, second, to establish what in effect if not in theory was a complete baronial oligarchy with the monarchy only retained as a figurehead. Men of the stamp of Lancaster and Warwick were not scheming politicians or subtle constitutional lawyers, they were fighting barons jealous of foreign upstarts and fearful of royal authority. True,

[1] For the *Ordinances* see Appendix II, pp. 158–61.
[2] *Vita*, 18–19.

they summoned the commons to approve their Ordinances, and in the twenty-ninth clause ordained that parliaments should be held at least once a year, but they did not say that the commons *must* be represented, and their proposals provided for the sanction of the baronage only.[1]

In addition to the exile of Gaveston, the Frescobaldi and some of the king's other personal friends, the Ordinances decreed that in future the magnates were to control the appointment of all the chief officials of the kingdom and of the royal household, that the king should not go to war or leave the realm without their consent, that the 'new custom', which was an extra duty on foreign merchants initiated by Edward I, was to be abolished together with all abuses of purveyance, and that all illegal 'prises' and 'Maltotes' should be 'utterly abolished forever'.[2] One historian has described these drastic decrees as 'a complete programme of limited monarchy – there was no reference to commons or clergy', and, if this is an exaggeration, it is certainly true that they were essentially a cloaking in technical constitutional language of a personal attack by the barons on a king they despised, and on an able royal favourite whose power had roused their jealousy and whose foreign wit had pricked their self-importance.[3]

The twentieth Ordinance, which condemned Gaveston to perpetual exile, decreed that he had to be out of the country by 1 November via Dover.[4] In the event, he was protected by the king, and sailed from the Thames on 3 November. The accounts of his travels during the next few weeks are inconsistent and unreliable – he may have gone to France first but he probably went direct to Flanders, where the king had influence through his sister Margaret, wife of the duke of Brabant. What is certain is that, before the end of the year 1311, Gaveston was back in England 'now in the king's apartments, now at Wallingford and now at Tintagel Castle'.[5] It was apparent that the king had no intention either of holding to any of the Ordinances or

[1] See J. Conway Davies, *op. cit.* 360–93.

[2] *Ordinances*, Clause XI.

[3] T. F. Tout, *The Political History of England, 1216–1377* (London, 1930), 248.

[4] *Rymer*, II, 144. Below Appendix II, p. 160.

[5] *Vita*, 21.

of giving up his friend. His evasions, and several of his household appointments in direct disregard of the Ordinances,
prompted the barons to issue a further document known as the
'Second Ordinances of the Earls'. It was published towards the
end of November 1311 before Gaveston's return was known,
and it is an elaboration of the penal personal clauses of the
original Ordinances naming many of the royal household
officials and personal friends who were also to be dismissed, and
ordering that Gaveston's family and household were also to be
exiled. Edward not surprisingly complained that he was being
treated 'as one would provide for an idiot', and he openly
entertained his 'Perrot' at his Christmas celebrations at
Windsor. A violent clash with the Lords Ordainers seemed
inevitable.[1]

On 20 January 1312, Edward restored Gaveston to his title
and properties, and Archbishop Winchelsey immediately
countered by declaring Gaveston excommunicate in accordance with the twentieth Ordinance.[2] The barons prepared for
civil war. The five earls took mutual oaths to defend the
Ordinances, even Gloucester signified reluctant approval, and
detailed secret plans were made for joint action. Under cover of
district tournaments, each of the earls was to organize armed
musters, and, as Edward and Gaveston were seeking safety in
the north, Lancaster with his private army followed them.[3]
Early in May 1312, Edward and Gaveston were at Newcastle,
and it was rumoured that an attempt to obtain ignominious
refuge with Bruce in Scotland had failed.[4] Lancaster's rapid
approach took the two friends by surprise, and the men of
Newcastle were in no heart to fight for them. Edward and
Gaveston just managed to avoid capture by Lancaster and
escaped to Tynemouth and thence by sea to Scarborough, but
had to leave behind not only large quantities of arms, treasure
and baggage but their households, including the pregnant
Queen Isabella who became Lancaster's prisoner. The king and
Gaveston now separated, and the reason is not quite clear.

[1] *Vita*, 21.
[2] *Rymer*, II, 153–4, 167.
[3] *Ann. Lond.*, 204.
[4] A stupid scheme ('inane studium') says *Vita*, 22.

Gaveston may have thought himself safe behind the walls of Scarborough's cliff castle, while the king may have been trying to raise reinforcements from headquarters at York. Lancaster, with unusual good sense, took up his position between the two friends, while Pembroke, Surrey, and Henry Percy laid siege to Scarborough Castle. The castle apparently was ill-prepared, and at the end of three weeks' siege Gaveston sued for terms. The terms granted were surprisingly generous. On 19 May 1312, Gaveston surrendered on condition that he himself would be allowed to plead his case before parliament, and that his men could retain the castle until August, and even revictual it in the meantime.[1] If no decision were forthcoming from parliament by the agreed date, Gaveston would be allowed to return to the castle. Pembroke, Surrey and Percy swore on the Host that they agreed to these terms, and Pembroke, apparently of his own accord, even pledged his honour and 'his lands and tenements' to the king as additional guarantee. Pembroke slowly escorted Gaveston south intending to deposit him under guard in Gaveston's own castle at Wallingford until proceedings in parliament could begin. Three weeks later, Pembroke and his prisoner reached the village of Deddington some ten miles south of Banbury. Pembroke decided to leave Gaveston there with his guards while he himself took the opportunity of spending the night with his wife, who was at Bampton about twelve miles farther on. Early on the morning of 10 June, the earl of Warwick, who had apparently been waiting for just such an opportunity, surrounded the rectory where Gaveston was sleeping, and took him prisoner before he was properly dressed. Gaveston was treated like a common malefactor and thrown into a dungeon in Warwick Castle.

Pembroke, on hearing of this unchivalrous act, was furious. He attempted to persuade Gloucester to help to set matters right, and received only a dusty answer. He appealed to the university and citizens of Oxford, and received an equally dusty answer. His honour was at stake, his estates were liable to forfeiture, and no one seemed to care. No one was ready to lend a hand to rescue the hated favourite, and Pembroke's own

[1] *Vita*, 24, *Ann. Lond.*, 205; *Bridlington*, 43.

8 Leeds Castle (Kent)

9 Aymer de Valence, earl of Pembroke

conduct in not guarding his prisoner with greater care was obviously blameworthy.

At this point the earls of Lancaster, Hereford and Arundel arrived at Warwick Castle. It was clear that their purpose was speedy and rough justice for Gaveston, but no one was over-anxious to take responsibility. They agreed that, as Gaveston was an earl, married to Gloucester's sister, he should not suffer a traitor's death but should be beheaded 'as a nobleman and Roman citizen'.[1] Gaveston was dragged off to Blacklow Hill, about two miles from Warwick on the way to Kenilworth, and within the estates of Lancaster. There, while the three earls watched from a distance, and in the absence of Warwick (the Black Hound of Arden preferred his kennel) Gaveston was murdered. A Welsh soldier ran him through the body with his sword, and another struck off the head, which he proudly took to Lancaster. Four cobblers took the headless corpse to the earl of Warwick but he refused to receive it, and later the remains found temporary refuge in the convent of the Dominicans in Oxford. They could not be buried in consecrated ground as Gaveston had died excommunicate.[2]

The death of Gaveston was the result of a disgraceful and unchivalrous breach of faith – for Warwick, Lancaster and Hereford as confederates of Pembroke, were all equally bound by the oaths taken at Scarborough. But was it simple murder? By the Ordinances, Gaveston had become an outlaw, and one version of the tragedy says that two justices actually sanctioned the execution.[3] No one save Lancaster was willing to accept final responsibility for the deed, and Gaveston's condemnation and death had been certain. Nevertheless, it was at best judicial murder, and undeniably a breach of a sacred oath – it was the beginning of two centuries of baronial slaughter.[4] The comment of an unknown northern chronicler writing some fifteen years later sums up admirably – 'Gaveston was wicked, impious and

---

[1] *Vita*, 26.

[2] *Ann. Lond.*, 206–7; *Flores Hist.*, III, 150–2.

[3] They were William Inge and Henry Spigurnel, *Bridlington*, 43–4.

[4] 'It was the first drop of the deluge which within a century and a half carried away nearly all the ancient baronage and a great proportion of the royal house of England'; W. Stubbs, *Constl. Histy. of England* (Oxford, 1906), II, 348.

criminal, and as such deserved to die. But the manner of his death was likewise wicked, impious and criminal. The men who inflicted his disgraceful death on Gaveston were themselves thereby disgraced. And it was a death especially to be deplored because later it was the excuse for the shedding of so much noble blood in the horrors of civil war.'[1]

It is difficult for a modern observer to see Gaveston clearly. He can look on what is probably the recumbent effigy of Gaveston's father in Winchester's retro-choir, but there is nothing more to reveal Gaveston himself. Clearly, he was a brave and efficient soldier, a more than capable jouster, and his short experience of administration in Ireland was to his credit. Naturally he enjoyed the lofty titles, the rich estate, the landed wealth and the precious jewels lavished upon him by Edward, and naturally he took good care of his Gascon relatives and friends, but he does not appear to have aspired to govern England – he was content to be the favourite of England's king. His chief offence was his lack of respect for great barons of established lineage, little culture and less wit who were simply jealous of his sudden rise to royal favour and fortune. It is significant that these English-born barons were hating him as a Gascon – their crude envy was a sign of burgeoning English nationalism which had first begun to appear when Edward's grandfather had favoured his Provençal relatives. It was Gaveston as the upstart foreigner rather than as the immoral pervert who was betrayed to death on Blacklow Hill.

[1] See G. L. Haskins in *Speculum*, XIV (1939), 76. I am greatly indebted to Sir J. G. Edwards for advice on the chronicler's almost untranslatable and therefore summarized verdict. The full text runs:
'O viri execrabilis, mors execrandi! O mors nepharii quam nephanda! O mors impii impiissima! O mors scelerati sceleratissima! Nec immerito est mors ejus tam vilis et reproba censenda, cuius pretexta tantus cruor et tam preciosus falso et maliciose effunditur subsequenter.'

Chapter 7

LANCASTER
AND
BANNOCKBURN

'I am certain the king grieved for Piers as a father grieves for his son. For the greater the love, the greater the sorrow. In the lament of David upon Jonathan love is depicted which is said to have surpassed the love of women. Our king also spoke thus; and further he planned to avenge the death of Piers.' That is the shrewd summing up of the observer who wrote the first biography of Edward II, and the remainder of Edward's reign is largely a commentary on this text.

Immediately he heard of Gaveston's murder, the king realized that he might profit from the inevitable split in the baronial caucus which had engineered it. He returned to London and ordered horses and weapons to be made ready; he went to Dover and pledged the seamen of the Cinque Ports to his aid; he sent Pembroke to seek help from Philip IV. Pembroke was naturally enraged at Lancaster and Warwick for soiling his honour, and even Surrey shared his disgust. Both were now prepared to work for the king. And Edward was not deprived of all his intimate personal friends – Sir Hugh Despenser (the elder) was back at his side, and Henry de Beaumont and Edmund de Mauley, in spite of Ordinances which had decreed their exile, were still at court.[1]

The three earls who had encompassed Gaveston's murder – Lancaster, Warwick and Hereford – had planned to march on London, but their action had been anticipated by the king; London's gates were shut and the Londoners had been warned

[1] *Vita*, 30–1; *Ann. Lond.*, 208–10.

73

to be on guard. The earls were forced to halt near Ware, some twenty miles north of the capital, and there, it was said, Lancaster had at least a thousand men-at-arms, Hereford a large contingent of Welsh soldiery from Brecon, and Warwick his armed retinue from the forest of Arden.[1]

There were hot-heads who counselled Edward to an immediate onset, but there were also wiser counsellors, amongst whom were Gloucester and several of the bishops, who urged caution, and who pointed out that the gravest threat to England at this time was not from over-mighty barons but from Robert Bruce and marauding Scots. An embassy from Clement V led by Cardinal Arnold of St Priscia, and French lawyers in the retinue of Louis, count of Evreux, who had been sent to Edward in answer to Pembroke's plea for help, were also on the side of compromise and peace. The king himself was in no hurry – he was anxious to have legal opinion in favour of his view that the Ordinances were *ultra vires*, and the death of Gaveston murder. The three earls were firm in their contrary view, yet equally reluctant to plunge hastily into the horrors of civil war. Lengthy peace negotiations were progressing when, on 13 November 1312, Queen Isabella gave birth to her first child.[2] The king was overjoyed, and his great grief over Gaveston was somewhat assuaged. He gave general pleasure by christening his heir Edward and not Louis, as some of his Francophile courtiers had suggested. Londoners were able to enjoy a week's free junketing to celebrate the birth, and negotiations for agreement between Edward and the earls were speeded up and occupied much of the time of the autumn parliament of 1312. The treasure[3] captured by Lancaster at Newcastle, when Edward and Gaveston had escaped to Scarborough, caused difficulties, but in February 1313 restoration was agreed. Yet final peace was still delayed – the earls stood by the Ordinances, and Edward stood by Gaveston, whom he refused to brand as a traitor.

In early May, the death of Archbishop Winchelsey, who had long been suffering from palsy, gave Edward the opportunity

[1] *Vita*, 32; H. T. Riley, *Memorials of London* (London, 1868), 102–4.
[2] *Ann. Lond.*, 220–1.
[3] For Gaveston's jewels see E. A. Roberts in *Camden Miscellany*, XV (1929); *Genesis*, I, 54; *Maddicott*, 131.

to appoint an archbishop who would be his ally. The chapter
of Canterbury had elected the very worthy Thomas Cobham,
but Edward had no difficulty in persuading the amenable Pope
Clement to approve the appointment of Walter Reynolds, who
was already, by royal favour, bishop of Worcester. There is no
doubt that Reynolds' preferment was grossly simoniacal – it
cost both Reynolds and Edward a great deal of money – and
there were many who shared the chronicler's view that Reynolds
was 'a mere clerk and scarcely literate'.[1] But the evidence for this
slander is slight – he had at least earned Edward I's approval.
He was at this time very much a partisan of the king, and a
very close intimate.

In late May, Edward decided to quit the peace negotiations
for a period, and, leaving Gloucester as his regent, he took
Isabella to France for the knighting of her three brothers. At
Paris and Pontoise the English delegation shared in the splendid
celebrations, and at Pontoise Edward and Isabella narrowly
escaped death in a fire which forced them to escape from the
palace in their night attire. They returned to England on 16
July, and negotiations for reconciliation with the barons were
speeded up. In Westminster Hall on 14 October 1313, the earls
of Lancaster, Hereford and Warwick at last made their public
apologies for the events surrounding the death of Gaveston, and,
in exchange, they and five hundred of their dependants
received full pardons and a promise that their grievances would
be redressed. The terms of this settlement made no reference
whatsoever to the Ordinances – which seemed a major victory
for Edward. Two banquets – one given by the king and the other
by Lancaster – celebrated the occasion; but it was in fact a
patching up of a division much too deep to be bridged by mere
parchment and sealing wax, and much too serious to be
forgotten in junketing.[2]

But Edward could now turn his attention to the north, where
Bruce's civil war had prospered, and his rebellion had made
considerable progress without interference from a very much
preoccupied England. During the English 'troubles' of 1312,

[1] *Bridlington*, 45; *Melsa*, II, 329; H. G. Richardson in *E.H.R.*, LVI
(1941), 99; *Vita*, 40, 45.
[2] *Rymer*, II, 230; *Vita*, 43–4; *Trokelowe*, 80–1; *Maddicott*, 137–54.

Bruce had recaptured Dundee and Perth. In 1313 he had regained Linlithgow and the Isle of Man. And throughout this period, raids across the Border – sometimes as far south as York– had never ceased. Bruce had no siege engines and no heavy cavalry, but he had brave guerrillas who never shrank from the hazards of night attacks, and were ever ready to lead their fellow clansmen in surprise forays, which used grappling hooks and light ladders with devastating effect. Most of the Comyn family had now joined Bruce, and at Dundee in February 1310 the Scottish clergy had formally recognized him as king. Castle after castle fell to him, but one of the greatest and certainly the most important – Stirling – was withstanding a long siege by Bruce's brother Edward. Sir Philip Mowbray, a Scot, was holding it for the English, and at midsummer of 1313 Mowbray was fortunate in obtaining a truce from Edward Bruce which infuriated his brother.[1] Unless an English relieving army came within three leagues of Stirling Castle before midsummer 1314, Mowbray would surrender – this gave the English a year to retrieve a situation which was becoming desperate. King Robert of Scotland, now forty years of age, could feel that at last he had the bulk of Scotland behind him, and he might be able to face invading English with a fair chance of success. The arrangement between Mowbray and his brother was not, however, to his liking. It might commit him to a pitched battle in the open, whereas his steady policy was to avoid this in favour of guerrilla tactics. To Edward and the English baronage, on the other hand, here was a chivalrous challenge which could not be ignored. Preparations for a major expedition against the Scots were put in hand – Edward would 'keep faith' with his father, divert disgruntled barons from their English discontents, and bring succour to the hard-pressed garrison of Stirling Castle and its gallant commander.

On 23 December 1313, writs of summons to military service in Scotland were sent to eight earls, including Thomas of Lancaster, and eighty-seven barons, naming Berwick as the rendezvous for 10 June 1314. It was to be a full-scale invasion by both sea and land by way of the eastern approaches. All English ports had to contribute ships and sailors, and Richard

[1] Barbour, *Bruce*, 191–2.

de Burgh, the earl of Ulster and Bruce's father-in-law, was commissioned to send barons, knights and native Irish.[1] The earls of Gloucester, Hereford and Pembroke were prompt to answer the summonses in person, but the earls of Lancaster, Warwick, Arundel and Surrey refused to attend, and sent only the minimum quotas of their feudal obligations. It proved the hypocrisy of the peace banquets in the previous October, and the Blacklow earls' only excuse was that, according to the Ordinances, the king should have consulted his barons before taking up arms – it was an excuse quite insufficient to erase the stain upon their honour.[2] Yet the king had the support of experienced soldiers – the elder Sir Hugh Despenser, Sir Henry de Beaumont, Sir Robert Clifford, Sir Maurice de Berkeley, Sir Marmaduke Tweng, Sir Pain Tiptoft and Sir Giles d'Argentan had all seen distinguished service in Welsh and Scottish wars. There was a welcome contingent of adventuring knights from overseas not only from Ireland but from Gascony, France and Germany. There were Scottish knights, too, like Sir Ingram de Umfraville and some of the Comyns, Macdougalls and MacNabs who had as yet refused to side with Bruce. Perhaps the most experienced soldier on either side was Aymer de Valence, earl of Pembroke. He had already met Bruce in two battles – he had defeated him at Methven in 1306 and lost to him at Loudoun Hill in 1307[3] – and he knew the difficulties of the Scottish terrain. Edward himself had behind him the experience of four full-scale Scottish campaigns – but he had not yet met Bruce.

Estimates of the size of the rival forces have varied widely, and this is not surprising when none of the authorities were eye-witnesses. Edward's biographer says that his cavalry 'numbered over 2,000 without counting a numerous crowd of infantry'. Barbour, with pardonable exaggeration in a Scot, says 40,000 horse of whom 3,000 were 'barded'. In modern times, Oman estimated 'near 3,000 horse' with 15,000 to 18,000 infantry, while Morris prefers '2,000 to 2,500 mounted troops.' Two more

[1] *Cal. Close Rolls 1313–18*, 86; J. E. Morris, *Bannockburn* (Cambridge, 1914), 40–1; Barbour, *Bruce*, 194 – 'a great meinie from Ireland'.
[2] *Vita*, 49–50; *Lanercost*, 206.
[3] C. Oman, *op. cit.* II, 83.

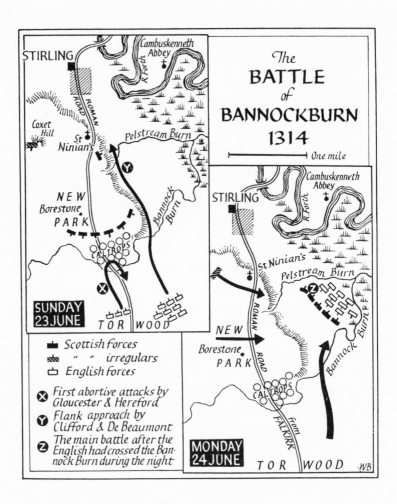

The
BATTLE
of
BANNOCKBURN
1314

One mile

Scottish forces
    "   "   irregulars
English forces

⊗ First abortive attacks by
    Gloucester & Hereford
Ⓨ Flank approach by
    Clifford & De Beaumont
Ⓩ The main battle after the
    English had crossed the Ban-
    nock Burn during the night

recent estimates in the one case give Edward 2,000 horse and 17,000 infantry, and in the other 2,500 horse and 15,000 infantry. In contrast, Bruce's army was naturally poorly supplied with the heavy 'destriers' of medieval cavalry, and his knights fought on foot with their retainers. Oman estimated Bruce's whole force at 10,000 at the most, while Barbour gave him 30,000 against the English 100,000. There was evidently a small body of Scottish light cavalry numbering about 500. The latest estimate of Bruce's army is between 7,000 and 10,000, of whom perhaps only 6,000 were in the lines of battle.[1] The consensus of much learned argument is that some 6,000 Scots were facing some 2,500 heavy English cavalry and about 15,000 English infantry. Both sides had archers, but neither side had large numbers of them – the era of the long-bow was only just beginning.

The battle which Edward and Bruce were about to fight is now named Bannockburn. It took some time for this name to gain general acceptance – early chroniclers refer to the 'battle of the Pools', or 'the battle near Stirling', or 'the field of Bannok', and the earliest-known reference to it is, curiously enough, in a Welsh chronicle which refers to a battle in 'y polles'. But within twenty-five years, the name 'Bannucksburne' was accepted, although the exact place of the main engagement has been in dispute to the present day. But at last the dust of controversy seems to be settling, and the tale of the battle of Bannockburn can now be told without too many notes to cover contrary opinions.[2]

The way from Falkirk to Stirling (some fifteen miles north) passed through the Torwood, consisting of wooded braes on slightly higher ground than the marshy creeks of the Forth and its tributary burns of Bannock and Pelstream to the east, and protected on the west by wilder and much higher moors. Bruce was not yet sure that he would risk a pitched battle; in the meantime hereabouts he picked an admirable site for his headquarters if he had to abandon his favourite guerrilla tactics and stand and fight. Today, the rotunda and modern romantic statue by the Borestone marks the likely spot where Bruce raised his standard. His men had excellent cover in, and a commanding view from, the higher forested land of what was known as the New Park, and there they barred the direct route

[1] *Vita*, 50; Barbour, *Bruce*, 194, 198; C. Oman, *op. cit.* II, 86–90; Bower, II, 248; G. W. S. Barrow, *Bruce, op. cit.* 295–6; M. McKisack, *The Fourteenth Century, op. cit.* 34–6; J. E. Morris, *Bannockburn, op. cit.* 40–1.

[2] G. W. S. Barrow, *Bruce, op. cit.* 301–10, 320–1; T. Miller, *The Site of the battle of Bannockburn*, Hist. Assoc. 1931; R. A. Carruthers' appendix to E. M. Barron, *The Scottish War of Independence* (Inverness, 1934); W. Mackay Mackenzie, *The Battle of Bannockburn* (Edinburgh, 1931); P. Christison, *Bannockburn; the story of the battle*, National Trust for Scotland, Edinburgh 1962.

to Stirling Castle, and could force the English either to a difficult frontal assault or to a hazardous flanking movement through the lower marshy ground between the Borestone and the estuary of the Forth. Bruce made frontal attack more difficult by digging pits (or 'caltrops') on either side of the way from the south to trap any unwary cavalry.[1]

The English army crossed the Tweed about 17 June, and the chroniclers remark on the enormous size of its commissariat – if the wagons 'had been lined up end to end they would have stretched for twenty miles'.[2] But this was a wise precaution – a policy of 'living off the country' would have been suicidal; they were right to take ample provisions and 'impedimenta' with them. The route north was through Lauderdale, and it took four days to reach Edinburgh, where more stores and equipment had arrived by sea at Leith. There was, however, not much time. If Stirling were not relieved by midsummer day, it must surrender. At this time of year in Scotland, there were probably twenty hours of daylight, and Edward determined to make the most of them – he decided to press on to Falkirk. It meant another exhausting march of over twenty miles, while Bruce's army was waiting in the comparative ease of their bivouacs.[3] Moreover, as the army approached the Torwood, on Sunday 23 June, there was some bickering among the English leaders. Edward had unwisely made his friend Gloucester constable for the occasion, whereas Hereford was hereditary Constable of England – who, then, was to lead the van? The quarrel was settled by Edward making them both joint commanders.[4]

At this point, Sir Philip Mowbray, the captain of the Stirling garrison, arrived, presumably by chivalrous permission of the Scots. He pleaded that, as the English were now well within the stipulated three leagues of Stirling Castle, there was no need for any battle. But the English captains were unwilling to be deprived of a victory which they thought would be easy and overwhelming, and Edward was right in judging that retreat

[1] Barbour, *Bruce*, 202.
[2] *Vita*, 50.
[3] Barbour, *Bruce*, 201–4.
[4] *Flores Hist.*, III, 158; *Vita*, 53.

now would be his ruin, whereas a major victory over Bruce could be a crushing answer to recalcitrant barons sulking at home. The English, tired and weary but still confident, pressed on.[1]

As the vanguard under Gloucester and Hereford approached the Scottish positions, Sir Henry de Bohun, Hereford's nephew, was one of the first to catch sight of the enemy at the edge of the wooded New Park. He even spotted Bruce himself – not in full armour on his war-horse but on a small grey in a mere hauberk with his helmet ringed by a glinting crown and only an axe at his saddle-bow. Bruce was probably inspecting his men and their positions, and certainly not yet expecting any major engagement. Bohun saw his chance of immortality – setting his great lance in rest, he charged the Scottish king. Bruce swerved, and, as the English knight thundered past, Bruce rose in his stirrups and dealt such a blow with his battle-axe that de Bohun fell dead with helm and head split in two.[2] The watching Scots were exultant at so triumphant and so skilful a taking of first-blood.

But Gloucester and Hereford did not halt the English advance, and in the ensuing mêlée Gloucester was unhorsed. The encounter was, however, indecisive. Gloucester managed to avoid capture, and the English vanguard withdrew to safety.[3]

While this rash action was taking place, a more sensible move was being made by a force of mounted men-at-arms under Sir Robert Clifford and Sir Henry de Beaumont. They skirted the main Scottish positions on the main approach to Stirling, and attempted to reach the castle by way of the lower ground to the east.[4] They were almost safely through, when the move was observed by the Scots, and Thomas Randolph, earl of Moray, immediately led his men to thwart it. They formed themselves into the famous Scottish array known as a 'schiltrom', which meant a hedge-formation of infantry bristling with twelve-foot spears, which could withstand a charge of the heaviest cavalry

[1] *Scalacronica*, 141; *Lanercost*, 207ff.
[2] Barbour, *Bruce*, 211.
[3] *Vita*, 51.
[4] *Scalacronica*, 141; *Lanercost*, 225; Barbour, *Bruce*, 206 ff.

providing its ranks were not previously broken by archery attack. The English could make no impression on Randolph's array, and they broke away, some of them riding on to Stirling Castle but most returning to the main body under Edward.[1] The first day of battle was nearly over, and the Scots had had the better of it – they had seen the personal triumph of their hero king in single combat, and they had repulsed two formidable attacks by heavy cavalry – the Scottish morale was understandably high. On the other hand, the English were tired after long forced marches, they had nothing to show for either of the preliminary bouts, and there was no obvious easy route to Stirling Castle – the English morale was understandably low.

Edward and Pembroke were now faced with a difficult decision. Honour demanded a battle on the morrow, but the Scots were holding an excellent position on higher ground athwart the way to Stirling. Frontal attack had been tried and had failed. A bold policy, however, could by-pass the New Park by crossing the Bannockburn and fighting a pitched battle – if Bruce dared – on the less boggy ground between the Bannockburn and the Pelstream Burn. After all, the English were far superior in numbers and equipment – if the Scots did at last stand and fight, they would be swept away. The fateful decision was taken to cross the Bannockburn during the night.

The dangerous crossing was made with the help of troops sent out from the Castle with planks and timbers to bridge the narrow tidal gullies, and there was fortunately no night-attack from Bruce. But it was a very short night, and by day-break the English army was still in the process of re-forming and preparing for a major battle. Either late the previous evening or during the night, a Scot who had deserted from the English – Sir Alexander Seton – arrived at Bruce's headquarters. He reported that the English were in poor heart, and urged on Bruce that now was his hour, he should attack immediately.[2] There was another Scot who still remained loyal to Edward – Sir Ingram de Umfraville – and who, knowing the mettle of his

---

[1] In this action Sir Thomas Gray was taken prisoner; his son, when in an Edinburgh gaol about 1355, wrote the *Scalacronica* account of the battle from his father's memories of it.

[2] *Lanercost*, 207; *Scalacronica*, 42; Barbour, *Bruce*, 219–20; *Vita*, 51–2.

countrymen and realizing the poor position of the English forces, urged Edward to delay.[1] Gloucester agreed with Umfraville, and Edward accused his young peer of cowardice.

Shortly after the day-break of midsummer's day 1314, it was Bruce who launched the first attack. He ordered his brother Edward Bruce to advance in 'schiltrom' formation, and, as the English knights rode at the Scottish spears, the young Gloucester was among the first to fall. 'They advanced like a thick-set hedge, and such a phalanx could not easily be broken', says Edward's biographer.[2] Bruce ordered Randolph, earl of Moray, and Sir James Douglas to follow and support his brother, while he himself still held his 2,000 picked men in reserve. There was only one weapon which could have broken the Scottish 'schiltroms', it was the long-bow. But the English archers were few, and hemmed in behind the heavy cavalry – and there was little room for manoeuvre. Someone realized what was necessary, and the English archers began to shoot from the flank and take toll of the 'schiltroms'. But it was an early example of 'too little, too late'. Bruce sent the only cavalry he had – 500 light horse under Sir Robert Keith – to scatter the English archers, and they succeeded beyond his hopes; the few English and Welsh archers, some of whose arrows had found English backs in the confused mêlée, were scattered.[3] Bruce now threw in his reserve, and the battle became a massacre. When the Scottish irregular infantry, who had been held behind on Coxet Hill to the west of the village of St Ninian's, saw that Bruce was in the ascendant, they could not be held back – they rushed into the mêlée to kill and plunder. The hard-pressed English thought a second Scottish army was upon them, and, when they saw the royal banner leaving the field, they broke and fled.

Edward's bodyguard had realized that the battle was lost, and they had rightly decided to save their king from death – or, still worse, from capture. The king protested – he had fought gallantly, had had one horse killed under him and had lost his shield – but Pembroke, and Sir Giles d'Argentan, who was of the king's bodyguard, insisted on escape. They surrounded

[1] Barbour, *Bruce*, 223.
[2] *Vita*, 52; *Lanercost*, 208; Barbour, *Bruce*, 231.
[3] Barbour, *Bruce*, 227–9.

Edward with a body of 500 knights and rode hard for Stirling
Castle. They left a battle which had become a rout – hundreds
of the escaping English were drowned in one or other of the
streams and ditches, and hundreds were cut off and drowned by
the tidal waters of the Forth. When d'Argentan saw that his
king was safely on his way to the Castle, he turned back, and,
remarking that he was not used to flight, threw himself into the
fight and died, 'the third best knight in Christendom', on the
Scottish spears.[1] At Stirling Castle, the king was rightly refused
entry by Mowbray – it would certainly have meant his capture,
and a fearsome ransom. The royal party probably turned south
and east, and by roundabout ways were just able to reach the
coast at Dunbar in spite of Douglas's attempts to overtake them.
There the king was able to find a ship which took him to
Bamburgh and thence to the comparative safety of Berwick,
where many of his gallant 500 joined him. Meanwhile, Hereford
and a large group of English knights had managed to reach
Bothwell Castle south of Glasgow. Its keeper allowed them
refuge, and then promptly handed them over as prisoners of
war to Bruce for future ransoming. A bare-foot Pembroke, and
many of his Welsh troops, had also escaped and found their
way to Carlisle over the bleak terrain of the Lowland moors.[2]
For Edward and the English 'the battle near Stirling 'was a
disaster without precedent; for Bruce and the Scots it was the
glorious prelude to independence.

From the military point of view, Bannockburn was as
significant as the battle of Courtrai just before it and the battle
of Morgarten just after it. At Courtrai in 1302 a Flemish citizen
army had defeated the mounted feudal arrays of France. At
Morgarten in 1315 Swiss peasants with their halberds had
massacred the heavy armoured cavalry of the Hapsburgs. These
three famous battles proved that the day of the mailed mounted
knights was over, and that men-at-arms on foot, if correctly

[1] *Scalacronica*, 142–3; Barbour, *Bruce*, 234–5; *Walsingham*, I, 141.

[2] Barbour, *Bruce*, 241–3, where Barbour says that the fleeing English
'had not leisure even to make water'. Pembroke's Welsh, suggests
Professor G. W. S. Barrow, *Bruce*, *op. cit.* 332, may have been responsible
for the fact that the earliest report of Bannockburn is in the chronicle of
Valle Crucis Abbey, cf T. Jones, *Brut y Tywysogion* (Cardiff, 1952), 123,
219.

placed and well protected by archers, were invincible. It remained for the next generation of English soldiery also to teach Europe that the Welsh long-bow was the final answer to feudal armour.[1]

At Bannockburn, Bruce had proved himself an able general – he had chosen an excellent position, and he had handled his numerically inferior forces with consummate skill. But it is unjust to blame only Edward II for the English defeat. He shared responsibility with experienced generals, and he himself fought gallantly. Overwhelming numbers had bred over-confidence – but Edward was not alone in underrating his opponents. He and all of his generation had still to learn the lessons of Falkirk and Courtrai, and it was necessity and not ingenuity which had forced Bruce's knights to fight alongside their men on foot. If the war-horse in battle was doomed, the long-bowed archer and the dismounted man-at-arms had not yet become accepted. Bannockburn was a sign-post, and Edward of Caernarvon should not be condemned for being no wiser than many of his distinguished contemporaries.[2]

Edward was faced with the mortification of returning to England a defeated commander-in-chief to meet a Lancaster whose position was now impregnable. The absence of the three Blacklow earls had not been responsible for Edward's defeat, but their smug satisfaction at news of it was a measure of their patriotism. This was a bitter moment for Edward, but Bannockburn was not so much the defeat of a leader as the defeat of an established military tactic now hopelessly out of date.

[1] C. Oman, *op. cit.* II, 98–9, 113–16, 239–41; *Vita*, 56; *Ann. Lond.*, 231; *Baker*, 7.

[2] The only eye-witness of the battle was Robert Baston, an English Carmelite who had been commissioned by Edward to celebrate his victory in verse. He was taken prisoner, and his rhymes are of little value; cf W. D. Macray in *E.H.R.*, XIX (1904), 507–8. The *Scalacronica* was written about 1355, and Barbour's *Bruce* in about 1375.

Chapter 8

THE BAD YEARS
AND
LANCASTER

The consequences of Bannockburn were disastrous for England. 'Alas, the sorrow and loss that there was done,' writes the Brut chronicler. 'No man could number' the slain, and King Edward was 'scomfitede'. Higden and his translator report that Edward was 'schameliche overcome' and 'fowle devicte at Stirling'.[1] The twenty-three-year-old earl of Gloucester was dead, leaving one of England's greatest earldoms to be divided between his three sisters, and so providing tinder for future civil wars. The earl of Hereford had been taken prisoner, and was judged so great a prize that Bruce was able to exchange him for his own queen Elizabeth, their daughter Marjorie, his sister Christine, and that old instigator of rebellion Robert Wishart, bishop of Glasgow. Sir Robert Clifford, the victor of Caerlaverock, Sir Edmund de Mauley, steward of Edward's household, Sir John Comyn, son of the victim of the murder at Dumfries were only three of the thirty or forty barons who had been slain or drowned. Sir Roger Northburgh, keeper of the king's privy seal and his shield-bearer – he had lost both seal and shield in the battle – was only one of hundreds of distinguished prisoners now in Bruce's hands. The chroniclers for once did not exaggerate.[2]

But in victory Robert Bruce showed himself surprisingly magnanimous. He kept a night's vigil over the bier of his

---

[1] *Brut*, I, 208; *Higden*, VIII, 304–5; *Ann. Lond.*, 231.

[2] *Ann. Lond.*, 231; *Scalacronica*, 142–5; Barbour, *Bruce*, 234, 240; *Walsingham*, I, 141, 142; G. W. S. Barrow, *Bruce*, op. cit. 290–322.

cousin Gloucester, and chivalrously dispatched it next day, together with the body of Clifford, to Edward at Berwick for burials alongside their ancestors. Edward's lost shield was courteously returned, several captured English knights, whom Bruce had known when he was serving Edward's father, were freed without ransom, and, after Stirling Castle was duly surrendered, its Scottish captain, Mowbray, was welcomed into Bruce's peace without rancour. Yet Bruce's victory, overwhelming as it was, must be seen in perspective. Edward II was not the only English commander defeated by Scots, and Bannockburn, it has been pointed out, was only the most outstanding of *many* English defeats.[1] There have been critics of Bruce, and of the Bruce myth, who have maintained with some justification that Bannockburn bore no better fruit for Scotland than 'the uncontrolled licence of a rude aristocracy, the fitful efforts of the crown to control that licence and the profound misery of its people'. However that may be, there is no doubt that, for both the English crown and the English people at the time, Bannockburn was unmitigated tragedy.[2]

And the years 1314 and 1315, as it happened, were years of floods, poor crops and even of famine and pestilence all over Europe. In the north of England, therefore, nature's exceptional harshness added to the constant 'frightfulness' of marauding Scots.[3] Sir Edward Bruce, Thomas Randolph earl of Moray and Sir James Douglas – the Scots called him 'the Good Douglas' – led savage raids which reached Furness in Lancashire on the west, went beyond Richmond in Swaledale and even on one occasion reached as far as the peninsula of Holderness on the east.[4] There is a lively account in the chronicle of Jean le Bel (which Froissart incorporated in the early pages of his own chronicles), which gives an eyewitness description of these guerrilla Scots. They rode light ponies, and they lived largely on oat cakes cooked on the iron girdle plates they carried with them. They took prisoners for ransom, drove away horses and

[1] J. Harvey, *The Plantagenets*, (London, 1963), 79.
[2] The quotation is from H. H. Lancaster in *Essays and Reviews* (Edinburgh, 1876), 9.
[3] H. S. Lucas, *The Great European Famine* in *Speculum*, V (1930), 342–77; *Vita*, 69–70; *Knighton*, I, 411; *Bridlington*, 47–8.
[4] *Lanercost*, 210–11, 216.

cattle, looted plate and treasure, fired and plundered, and
ruthlessly levied blackmail.[1] A modern scholar has estimated
that, even by a conservative reckoning, Bruce's income from
these raids over a period of ten years reached £20,000 – an
enormous sum for fourteenth-century Scotland.[2] More orthodox
military excursions were, however, less successful. The larger
English castles were stubbornly defended, Richmond never
fell and Berwick resisted until 1318. Bruce himself, unsuccessful
in an attack on Carlisle in 1315, was defeated by the sheriff of
Cumberland, that Sir Andrew Harclay of Kirkby Stephen who
was soon to achieve greater fame. But for three years after the
battle of Bannockburn, England north of the Tees almost
ceased to be English – it was constantly overrun, and not a few
renegade local gentry turned freebooters as fearsome as the
Scots. Sir Gilbert Middleton of Mitford Castle in Northumberland, for example, even robbed two cardinals who were on a
papal peace-making embassy, and later paid for this, and many
more crimes, on the scaffold.[3] It is not to be wondered at that in
these years some northerners lost patience with the distant and
forgetful south, and decided to fight the Scots on their own
account. They gathered ships in the Humber and sailed to a
foolhardy invasion of Fife which, of course, failed – the Yorkshiremen were driven into the sea.[4]

Meanwhile, the Scots had become strong enough to risk
adventure across St George's Channel. In March 1315, Edward
Bruce and many other Bannockburn veterans, including
Thomas Randolph earl of Moray, sailed to Larne in Ulster to
attempt a conquest of Ireland. There were some who unkindly
suggested that Robert Bruce was not sorry to see a possible rival
out of his way, and others, more kindly, who suggested that the
Bruces were hoping to make Ireland a springboard for a flank
invasion of England through Celtic Wales. The expedition was
at first astonishingly successful, and within twelve months
Edward Bruce was crowned king of Ireland on a hill near

[1] See Appendix III, p. 162.
[2] J. Scammell in *E.H.R.*, LXXIII (1958), 402.
[3] *Vita*, 82–3; *Scalacronica*, 148; *Bridlington*, 52; *Maddicott*, 204–6.
[4] Barbour, *Bruce*, 292–6; *Bower*, II, 259.

Dundalk just south of the mountains of Mourne.[1] In the autumn of 1316, Robert went over with reinforcements to join his brother. Together they took fire and sword as far south as Limerick, but this was the limit of their successes. Gradually, the Scots were pushed back by Sir John de Bermingham, who on 14 October 1318 defeated and killed Edward Bruce at a battle by the hill of Faughart near Dundalk – his brother had already returned to Scotland. Bermingham was rewarded with the new earldom of Louth, the Scots retreated to Scotland, and some half-hearted attempts were made to reconcile the native Irish to the renewed English occupation. In the Annals of Ulster, the death of Edward Bruce was hailed as the greatest deed in Irish history, and, in describing the general devastation of the whole country, the annalist solemnly adds that 'people undoubtedly used to eat each other throughout Ireland'.[2] Ireland already had good cause to hate both English and Scots.

It was a bleak prospect for Edward II when, in early September 1314, he left Berwick to meet Lancaster and the rest of the Ordainers at York. Gloucester was dead, Hereford and Pembroke had nearly lost their lives and certainly much of their reputation and prestige, Warwick was self-important but ailing, Warenne of Surrey had degenerated into a despised lecher – there was now no possible rival to Thomas, earl of Lancaster, and Edward and his friends knew it. The biographer reports that the king 'refused nothing to the earls',[3] which meant that Lancaster's thesis that Bannockburn was the penalty for not carrying out the Ordinances had to be accepted, and that Lancaster now had *carte blanche* to attempt to enforce them in any way he wished. The first chapter of his programme was to change the administration. Archbishop Walter Reynolds was deprived of the Great Seal in favour of John Sandale soon to become bishop of Winchester, and Sir Walter Norwich succeeded Sandale as Treasurer – both the newcomers were

---

[1] E. Curtis, *History of Medieval Ireland* (Dublin, 1938), 178–201; Robert Dunlop in *Essays presented to T. F. Tout* (Manchester, 1925), 277–90; *Vita,* 61; Barbour, *Bruce,* 335.

[2] *Annals of Ulster,* Rolls Series, II, 433.

[3] *Vita,* 57 and 62.

Lancaster's men. All the sheriffs were changed 'according to the tenor of the Ordinances', and a start was made in re-organizing the king's household in Lancaster's favour.[1] The keeper of the king's wardrobe, Ingelard Warley, was dismissed, and replaced by William Melton, who in the following year became archbishop of York, and the purge continued to include John Ockham and many other royal household officials.

Edward found cold comfort in turning aside to remember his murdered 'Perrot'. Shortly after Christmas 1314, he made arrangements for an impressive funeral. Gaveston's remains were still with the black friars at Oxford, and Edward had provided funds for their proper care. Now, he arranged for Gaveston's final resting place – it was of course to be at Langley. The king, the archbishop of Canterbury, four bishops, fourteen abbots but, significantly, not many of the barons, attended an impressive ceremony in the church of the Dominicans which Edward had endowed at Langley. Royal funds financed masses for Gaveston's soul in churches all over England, and his family was also remembered. His widow was well provided for, and their only child Joan was duly found a suitable husband in the heir to the lord of Egremont.[2] Edward's love of Gaveston was deep, and the day of his revenge seemed no nearer.

A few weeks later, Edward's humiliation went even further – Walter Langton, Edward's old enemy who had since become his firm supporter, and the elder Sir Hugh Despenser, who had been one of Edward's chief ministers ever since his accession, were compelled to retire. The Ordinances exiling Henry de Beaumont, the foreign friend whom Edward had made king of Man, and his sister the lady de Vescy, were also enforced.[3] The king in 1315 was very much isolated.

All England was in a parlous state – and Lancaster was not the man to put things right. He was in a position of supreme authority and unbridled power, but even his supporters found him idle and irresolute, and he preferred to exercise his influence from a distance through lesser vassals and officials.

There was renewed trouble in Wales. Llewelyn Bren, who

[1] Tout, *Place*, 95–6; *Rot. Parl.*, I, 351–2.
[2] *Ann. Lond.*, 232; *Vita*, 58; J. Conway Davies, *op. cit.* 85–6.
[3] *Vita*, 57–8.

had been an important official of the dead earl of Gloucester, had resented an order which subordinated him to one Payne of Turberville. Unable to find satisfaction through the royal courts, Bren took to arms. Gathering a small army of supporting Welshmen, he attacked the great castle of Caerphilly. He was unable to take it but he did considerable damage before he was forced to retreat and seek safety in the Welsh mountains. The lately released earl of Hereford and other great Lords Marcher, including the Mortimers, were needed to suppress the revolt, and Bren only surrendered in the hope that thereby his men might find mercy. He himself found none – he was thrown into the Tower, where he remained for two years until he finally suffered all the agonies of a traitor's death at Cardiff.[1]

There was civil war even in Lancaster's own territories. Adam Banaster, an official of his household, had killed a man in a private quarrel, and he had little hope of pardon. He therefore ingeniously decided to exploit the known differences between Lancaster and the king. He posed as Edward's supporter, and hoped to earn royal favour and pardon by staging an armed rising in south Lancashire against Lancaster's local representative and friend Sir Robert Holland. Banaster attacked Liverpool, and he even stole a royal standard from a church to lend authority to an attack on Manchester. But his 800 men could not long withstand Holland's very superior forces; Banaster bravely fought to the death, and his head was sent to the earl. The rising was the excuse for savage reprisals by the brutal Holland.[2]

There was disorder, too, on the central Welsh border. The able royal household official Sir John Charlton was in dispute with the Lancastrian Griffith de la Pole over the lordship of Powys, and a lengthy and complicated legal issue, which involved both Welsh and English law, had been abandoned in favour of naked force. Griffith was pardoned in October 1316 thanks only to the influence of Lancaster.[3]

---

[1] *Vita*, 66–9; *Flores Hist.*, III, 339–40 and 343; *Bridlington*, 67–8; J. Conway Davies, *op. cit.* 31–2.

[2] *Ann. Paul.*, 279; *Vita*, 64–6; *Ann. Lond.*, 236–7; *Bridlington*, 48; *Flores Hist.*, III, 172–3; J. Conway Davies, *op. cit.* 504–5; Maddicott, 138–41.

[3] *Ibid.*, 216–17, 418; Maddicott, 174–7.

In Bristol, at this period the second city of England, there was open warfare for three years. The mass of the citizens had risen in revolt against the oligarchy of fourteen self-appointed leaders. Civic disorder had resulted in a royal judicial inquiry at which judgment had been given in favour of the fourteen, and Lord Badlesmere, a Kentish knight who was warden of Bristol Castle, supported the judgment. The citizens of Bristol, believing that the judges had been bribed by Badlesmere, had now no alternative but a resort to force. In a bloody riot, twenty men were killed, and the judges fled for their lives. At the inquest which followed at Gloucester eighty Bristolians were outlawed – a sentence which drove their fellows to even greater fury. The fourteen oligarchs were expelled, and for over two years Bristol was in a state of war. In 1316 so great a baron as the earl of Pembroke had to begin a full-scale siege, and only his huge siege-engines finally reduced the obstinate townsfolk to surrender.[1]

And Lancaster could not even keep order in his own intimate family circle. His wife Alice de Lacy, who had brought him three earldoms and vast properties, no longer wished to live with him. In May 1317 she deserted Lancaster, and, protected by Warenne, earl of Surrey, went to live with an obscure squire named L'Estrange whom she later married. Private war broke out, and Lancaster stormed the Yorkshire castles of Warenne.[2] It was said that the king had connived at the countess's elopement, and private local war seemed likely to develop into general civil war. Twice, royal forces were summoned to Yorkshire ostensibly to restore order, and Lancaster did not hesitate to put every obstacle in the way of their mobilization. At one point, Edward and the royal forces were at York while Lancaster and his private army were at his castle at Pontefract twenty miles to the south – well placed to bar Edward's return to London.[3] A collision seemed inevitable, but neither side was willing to take the first fatal step. Edward marched his men in full fighting order close by Pontefract Castle, but Lancaster did

[1] cf. Tout, *Place*, 93 ff.

[2] *Flores Hist.*, III, 178–9; *Melsa*, I, 335; *Ann. Paul.*, 280; *Bridlington*, 54; *Vita*, 87; J. Conway Davies, *op. cit.* 502–3; Tout, *Place*, 99.

[3] *Vita*, 81; *Bridlington*, 50–2; *Maddicott*, 210.

not accept the challenge. A final reckoning between the two was postponed.

In July 1314, Lancaster had been in an impregnable position. At the Lincoln parliament of February 1316 his triumph had been recognized – he had officially been made head of the king's council and commander-in-chief.[1] Yet by the end of the year 1318 his lease of power was clearly threatened, and his name and fame were discredited. Bruce had at last taken Berwick, the Ordinances were still not completely implemented, and a contemporary observer noted the disastrous state of stalemate between the rival forces of king and earl.[2] Edward had done all he could to exploit the baronial quarrels, but he was not yet strong enough to seek his final revenge. Lancaster had failed to make the most of his opportunities, and his supine incompetence had prepared the way for new leadership – it was soon to displace him.

[1] *Rymer*, II, 287; *Rot. Parl.*, I, 350–2; *Vita*, 69; Tout, *Place*, 94–9; A. Hughes in *T.R.H.S.*, X (1896), 41–58; H. Johnstone in *E.H.R.*, XXXVI (1925), 53–7.
[2] *Vita*, 75.

Chapter 9

PEMBROKE
AND
COMPROMISE

In an age when the English baronage was distinguished by some of its least attractive personalities, it is refreshing to find one who would have stood out in any age for his loyalty, his moderation and his intelligence – such a one was Aymer de Valence. He became earl of Pembroke through his mother, and, as a son of the Poitevin half-brother of the king's grandfather Henry, he was by birth close to the blood royal. He was some sixteen years older than the king, and had seen much service in the Scottish wars. As lieutenant of the Border, he twice met Bruce in the field – once in victory and once in defeat. In affairs of state he was no sycophant – he opposed Gaveston, who sneered at him as 'Joseph the Jew', and he had been one of the Lords Ordainers. He led the baronial army which besieged Gaveston in Scarborough Castle, and he was responsible for the generosity of the surrender terms. When Warwick, Lancaster and Hereford engineered the capture and judicial murder of Gaveston in contravention of a sacred oath, Pembroke broke with his baronial friends – he was enraged at the insult to his honour, and, although always genuinely a supporter of the Ordinances, he never forgave Lancaster.[1] For two years prior to Bannockburn, he shared with the elder Sir Hugh Despenser much of the day-to-day administration of the realm. His efficiency was never in question, and there was no record of any personal quarrel with Edward. He was at Edward's right hand on the Bannockburn campaign, and he especially distinguished himself in the

[1] See *supra* cap VI, pp. 70–1.

94

retreat. Like his king, he returned defeated to an England where a non-co-operative Lancaster and his allied earls were now supreme – he was quite content to step into the wings while their dreary play had its run. When Lancaster's incompetence became manifest, when Warwick died prematurely, when Surrey and Hereford proved of little weight and had quarrelled with Lancaster, it was to Pembroke that many turned as the only possible successor to the Blacklow earls.[1] Once again he and the elder Despenser were to share supreme power.

The elder Despenser also had been a distinguished and honoured servant of Edward I. Although his father fought for Simon de Montfort against the crown, and was killed at the battle of Evesham, Sir Hugh had become a favourite minister of Edward I, and, in due course, was ranked by Edward of Caernarvon, when Prince of Wales, as one of his personal older friends. He had long experience of war in Flanders and in Scotland, he had been on important diplomatic missions (including the one which arranged the royal French marriages) and he had been an able administrator in the king's household. During the Gaveston 'troubles' he was the only baron of the front rank to support the king throughout – a loyalty which earned him the undying hatred of Lancaster but the unfailing gratitude of Edward II. At Bannockburn, as one of Edward's bodyguard, he helped his escape to Dunbar, and, like Pembroke, on returning to England he found his old position untenable in the face of a triumphant Lancaster. He and Walter Langton were forced into retirement in 1315, when Lancaster began a purge of the royal administration in favour of his own personal supporters. But although hated by Lancaster, he was married to Warwick's sister and Warwick, just before he died shared much of Lancaster's power and influence. The elder Despenser's return to Court was therefore not long delayed, and an otherwise critical chronicler had to admit he was 'one of the most distinguished men of his day both in judgment and in probity'. The record proves that in his loyalty to his king Despenser was exceptional – he stood by him throughout his reign and served

[1] For Pembroke's career, see J. Conway Davies, *op. cit.* 110–12 and 322–31 and Tout, *Place*, 17–19.

him devotedly to the death. The elder Despenser was in many ways a worthy coadjutor to Aymer de Valence.[1]

Towards the end of 1317, tension between Edward and Lancaster was mounting towards a disastrous confrontation. Lancaster suspected that Edward was behind his private domestic troubles, and Edward was not alone in suspecting Lancaster of treasonable dealings with the Scots – the truth may have been that Edward was pleased to see any setback to the fortunes of the man he now regarded as his greatest enemy. And many observers noticed that the Scots' raids into England, which had been continuous since Bannockburn, 'left the earl's estates untouched', and it was suggested that Lancaster was fully prepared to ally himself with King Robert if ever he needed help against his own king.[2] Many of the barons, including such close collaborators of Lancaster as Hereford, were now ready to welcome moderation in an atmosphere which was increasingly thunderous – they rightly looked to Pembroke.

Two years before, Pembroke was sent with an embassy to the pope to seek aid against Bruce, and to discuss the thorny age-old problems of clerical taxation. With him went several bishops and Bartholomew lord Badlesmere, a kinsman of the late earl of Gloucester, who had been very much involved in the Bristol disorders. On the way home, Pembroke was kidnapped by a French knight who claimed that Edward owed him money for military services, and who thought that, with so distinguished a hostage, he might blackmail the king into paying his claim. He was right: Edward was never a laggard in supporting his friends, and, with the aid of his Italian bankers, he paid Pembroke's considerable ransom of £2,500. The earl was released after a few months' 'house arrest' in Germany.[3] It is thought that it was on this embassy that Pembroke and Badlesmere began the organization of an alliance which historians have labelled 'The Middle Party'. Whatever its origins, the

[1] J. Conway Davies, *op. cit.* 86–90 and 98–9; *Genesis*, I, 112–14. The quotation is from *Bridlington*, 87.

[2] *Vita*, 76; J. Conway Davies, *op. cit.* 424.

[3] *Murimuth*, 26; *Rymer*, II, 329–30; Tout, *Place*, 102–3.

label itself has to be used with reservations – it suggests too much of later political practice, and it connotes too much of official mechanism. On the other hand, it is a fact that the king could soon counter Lancaster with the help of a group of distinguished men, who included not only the elder Despenser and Reynolds archbishop of Canterbury, but also the earls of Pembroke, Hereford, Surrey, Arundel, and the king's young half-brother Thomas of Brotherton, now earl of Norfolk, together with such friendly bishops as Stapledon of Exeter and Langton of Chichester, such younger barons as the younger Despenser, Roger Damory, Hugh Daudley and William de Montague, and such powerful Lords Marcher as Roger Mortimer of Chirk and his nephew, Roger Mortimer of Wigmore. And there is extant a secret indenture, dated 24 November 1317, which was sealed by Pembroke and Badlesmere on the one hand and by Roger Damory on the other, by which Damory was pledged in the huge sum of £10,000 to support the other two as chief counsellors of the king.[1] It is possible that this is only one of a series of similar indentures binding the so-called 'Middle Party' into some kind of formal cohesion.

What were the aims of this new group? They were neither original nor revolutionary. Each of its members had personal ambitions to achieve or personal animosities to assuage. Pembroke wanted revenge for the betrayal at Deddington. The younger Despenser, Damory and Daudley were jealous of each other's shares in the Gloucester inheritance – each had married one of the three Gloucester co-heiresses. The surviving Blacklow earls were beginning to tire of Lancaster's personal supremacy. The Lords Marcher were suspicious of the aggressions of the Despensers and equally jealous of the power of Lancaster. Both the Despensers were now curialists in search of greater personal fortunes. The clergy naturally gave their allegiance where their preferments had originated. All were united only in their dissatisfaction with Lancaster's lack of leadership, yet they had no intention of ousting him from his rightful place in the national administration, providing he was prepared to do his duty and to share its responsibilities with his peers, and most of them,

---

[1] Doc. No. 42 in Appendix to J. Conway Davies, *op. cit.* 563–4 and 453–4. See also *ibid.*, 425–43; Tout, *Chapters*, II, 205 ff.; Tout, *Place*, 105–6.

including Pembroke, had no intention of releasing Edward from the strait-jacket of the Ordinances.

To the king, the 'Middle Party' was of course, welcome. He might be able to exploit its internal jealousies and differences, even if he had in the meantime to swallow some of its new remedies, and any move which thwarted Lancaster was a move towards that revenge for which he never ceased to hope.

The first objective of the 'Middle Party' was to encourage a *rapprochement* between the king and Lancaster, which would relax the position of tense stalemate. A series of conferences were held, beginning at Leicester, which were a sad commentary on the political state of England at this time. Lancaster was almost accorded the status of an independent prince, and it was only his own peculiar attitude of wanting power without its duties which prevented him from still holding on to the position he had held since Bannockburn. In April 1318, points of agreement were at last established – the Ordinances would be enforced and maintained, Edward's evil counsellors would be dismissed, Lancaster and his friends would receive pardons for any legal trespasses, and the prospects for a meeting between principals seemed bright. Haggling over details between Lancaster and the Pembroke group continued through the summer, but at last it was Lancaster's own suggestion for a standing baronial council which brought final agreement. On 9 August 1318, a 'treaty' was sealed at Leake, just south of Nottingham, which was actually an indenture between Lancaster and the leaders of the 'Middle Party', and it is significant that it has always been called a 'treaty' – it seemed to be an agreement between hostile sovereign states.[1]

The 'treaty' of Leake at first sight might appear to have given Lancaster most of what he wanted. The Ordinances were again approved, and even given additional sanctity by being read out in the good company of Magna Carta. They would be strictly adhered to, and Lancaster and his friends duly received

---

[1] B. Wilkinson in *Studies presented to F. M. Powicke* (Oxford, 1948), 333–53; J. G. Edwards in *Essays presented to R. L. Poole* (Oxford, 1927), 360–78; *Vita*, 88; *Knighton*, I, 413–21; *Rymer*, II, 370; *Rot. Parl.*, I, 453–5; Tout, *Place*, 110–12; J. Conway Davies, *op. cit.*, 447–50; *Genesis*, I, 92.; *Maddicott*, 226–9.

their pardons. Parliament would be summoned to authorize all these arrangements, and a standing council would be appointed which would always include one member nominated by Lancaster. This standing council would control the king's every act, and in effect would govern the realm through a standing committee of two bishops, one earl, one baron and one Lancastrian banneret. But it was soon apparent that Lancaster had been out-manoeuvred. He was not himself to be a member of the governing council – possibly by his own preference for idleness – and his representative was a mere banneret who would have no power of veto. The major council was to consist of eight bishops, four earls, four barons and Lancaster's banneret, and it was of course to be preponderantly 'Middle Party'. A few days after the meeting at Leake, Edward met Lancaster on the bridge over the river Soar at Hathern near Loughborough, and the customary kisses of peace were exchanged. There was only one cloud in the summer sky – Lancaster still refused to be reconciled with the elder Despenser, and he also reserved his right to pursue his private quarrel with Surrey. Lancaster had been replaced by Pembroke, but the king was chained to a new piece of machinery entirely in the control of bishops and baronage. There was nothing as yet which Edward could do but accept the new situation gracefully in the hope that soon he might find in the new machinery's working some opportunity to further his own interests. It is at this low ebb in Edward's fortunes that it is not surprising to find rumours of pretenders claiming that Edward was a supposititious child. One claimant, who appeared at Oxford, was later condemned to a traitor's death. But if Edward's wings were still grievously clipped, Lancaster was in no better plight.

On 28 October 1318 at York, a parliament began its sittings, which was called primarily to regularize the proceedings at Leake. Surrey and the elder Despenser tactfully stayed away,[1] but otherwise there was a full muster of the protagonists of both sides even including Lancaster. The governing council was enlarged to include the younger Despenser, Badlesmere and

[1] In *Vita*, 93 it is hinted that Despenser took the opportunity to make a pilgrimage to the shrine of St James at Compostella. For the 'treaty' see *Stat.*, I, 177.

some others, and a special committee was appointed to reform the royal household.[1] The sheriffs were all discharged and replaced, and negotiations were begun on complicated matters connected with scutage. But the most important acts of this parliament were the endorsement of the younger Despenser's appointment as Edward's chamberlain, and the substitution of Badlesmere for William de Montague as Edward's steward – de Montague was promoted to be seneschal of Gascony. It was Badlesmere's appointment which must have made it clear to Lancaster how far the mighty had fallen. As earl of Leicester through his wife, Lancaster in 1308 had been confirmed as hereditary Steward of England. He now claimed that, exactly as the hereditary Marshal of England nominated the marshal of the royal household, so he, as hereditary Steward, should have the right to nominate the royal steward, and therefore control a key post at the very centre of power. It was a claim with some logic behind it but no history, and was parried by a promise to search the records for precedents.[2] Meanwhile, Badlesmere continued to hold the office. Similar delaying tactics were used when Lancaster raised the same question at another parliament at York in the following year, and with the same negative results. Badlesmere remained royal steward, and he, Pembroke and the elder Despenser had replaced the earl of Lancaster, while the younger Despenser, who had once counselled the Lords Ordainers, was now a baronial renegade increasingly in the royal confidence.

In theory, as a result of the 'treaty' of Leake and the two parliaments of York, Edward's position at the beginning of the year 1319 as reigning monarch was a travesty of what the fourteenth century understood by monarchy. But Edward must be given credit for seeing that for a while he had nothing to lose by seeming to work willingly with the new machinery. He had at least counter-balanced Lancaster, and Pembroke and the new men who were now managing his affairs included many congenial friends – both the Despensers were now in his harness – and he even had no personal objections to the committee

[1] Tout, *Place*, 244 ff.

[2] Tout, *Place*, 96–7; L. W. Vernon Harcourt, *His Grace the Steward* (London, 1907), 124–6; *Maddicott*, 233, 241–3, 289–90.

which was about to investigate his household. A new era seemed to the chroniclers to be ushering in a new prosperity, and at last domestic strife would be abandoned so that a united effort could be made to settle the Scottish problem. All over Europe there was an end to the disastrous periods of dearth and pestilence, which had seemed to many to be divine retribution for the sins and failings of mankind. England, the chroniclers hoped, was again to enjoy adequate harvests, and a regime in which the leading administrators commanded the respect of their king and most of their peers.[1]

In June 1319, a muster of the fighting forces of the land was therefore summoned to Newcastle. Unlike the Bannockburn campaign, it was to be a truly nation-wide effort, and it was remarkable that both Thomas earl of Lancaster and his brother and presumptive heir, Henry, were there, and that they had no objections to the presence of the elder Despenser and of Surrey. The first objective was the recapture of Berwick, now defended by Walter the Stewart with Sir James Douglas commanding Bruce's hobelars in the offing. At the end of July, Edward and Pembroke, with some 8,000 well-armed troops and ample siege-engines sent by sea, mounted a full-scale siege of the famous border town. Bruce's strategy was brilliant. While the Stewart ably defended town and castle, Douglas and Murray were dispatched with their ruthless hobelars to cut the English supply routes farther south. A spy reported to the English at York that the Scots were aiming also at the capture of Edward's queen Isabella, and she was hastily sent south by water to the comparative safety of Nottingham. The Yorkshiremen now had to face wild and skilful marauders while the nation's best troops were fully occupied some 150 miles away at Berwick. The citizens and clergy of York formed themselves into an irregular militia, and under the leadership of William Melton, archbishop of York, they marched out bravely to face Douglas and Murray. They met at Myton in Swaledale, a few miles east of Boroughbridge, and in a most unequal contest the Yorkshiremen were routed. Many priests were among the slain and the drowned, and the battle therefore became known as 'The Chapter of Myton' or, on account of the large number of

[1] *Vita*, 90; H. S. Lucas in *Speculum*, V (1930), 343–77; *Bridlington*, 48.

white-habited monks present, 'The White Battle of Myton'.[1] The archbishop escaped with difficulty while the Scots pushed on to Pontefract – Lancaster's chief stronghold – and then proceeded to harry to the west of the Pennines on their way back to Scotland. It was no reflection on Edward that by general consent the siege of Berwick was abandoned so that the troops could hurry south to defend their homes. It was a sad end to a national effort, and a setback to the prospects of the 'Middle Party'. The best that Edward and Pembroke could manage was a two-year truce with Bruce.[2]

But the person who came off worst from the abortive Berwick expedition and the disaster at Myton was Lancaster. Again there was talk of treason. The elder Despenser was one of those who alleged that Lancaster had informed the Scots of the queen's presence in York, and there were others who alleged, less convincingly, that Lancaster had received £40,000 from Bruce 'to lend him secret aid', and that Lancaster's forces could, and should, have cut off Douglas's hobelars as they made for home. These slanders soon reached the ears of the earl, and he promptly offered to clear himself by the ancient ordeal of the white-hot iron. Instead, he was allowed to prove his innocence by compurgation – the sworn oaths of some of his peers. The king's biographer was still not satisfied; he records that, during the siege of Berwick, the king himself had suspected Lancaster of a treasonable half-heartedness, and that the king had been heard to remark that 'when this wretched business is over, we will turn our hands to other matters. For I have not yet forgotten the wrong that was done to my brother Piers', and the chronicler adds 'If the truth be told, the earl perhaps hindered that expedition'.[3] The optimistic and hypocritical mood of Leake was rapidly deteriorating.

In January 1320, a parliament was again summoned to York, and this time Lancaster refused to attend – his short period of full co-operation was over. The parliament was chiefly concerned

---

[1] *Scotichronicon*, 147–8; Barbour, *Bruce*, 304–10; *Brut*, I, 211–12.

[2] During this truce, the now-celebrated Declaration of Arbroath was dispatched, but neither Edward II nor most of his contemporaries can have heard of it. cf. B. Wilkinson *The Later Middle Ages in England* (London, 1969), 123; G. W. S. Barrow, *Bruce*, *op. cit.* 424–30.

[3] *Vita*, 97–102 and 104. For a kinder view see *Maddicott*, 249–50.

10 Brass to Sir John Creke and wife, c. 1325
(illustrating contemporary costume)

11 Isabella and the execution of Hugh le Despenser

with some ministerial changes prior to the king's approaching visit to France, where he was now overdue to render homage to Philip V, the new king of France, for Aquitaine and Ponthieu. In his absence, Pembroke was to act as regent, and Badlesmere was to be constable of Dover and warden of the Cinque Ports. On 19 June Edward left for Amiens, where the ceremonies were to take place, and, fortunately for Edward's reputation, a full account has survived of his conduct during the negotiations which followed. As a diplomatist he distinguished himself – he is reported as speaking with skill, great clarity and effective ability without the prompting of officials.[1] After a few weeks of feasting and ceremonial at Amiens, Edward returned to England, having crushed a mutiny in Abbeville, the chief town of Ponthieu, on his way. During the following months he took pains to show all his baronage that he now relied not so much on Pembroke and Badlesmere as on the two Despensers, and it was the younger who soon became almost as much of a royal confidant as Gaveston had been.

This younger Sir Hugh Despenser was a contemporary of Edward's. He had been knighted on the same day, he had been a member of the king's household since Edward was Prince of Wales and he had become the king's chamberlain in 1313.[2] Unlike his father, he had opposed Gaveston, and in 1308 he had been credited with inventing the 'doctrine of capacities', which threatened the king while safeguarding the throne, and in 1311 he was with the Lords Ordainers. After the death of the earl of Gloucester at Bannockburn, the king had given him the hand of the eldest of the three Clare co-heiresses, and received him back into royal favour. By 1317, the huge Gloucester estates in the south-east of Wales were divided into three, one part for each of the husbands of the three heiresses. Despenser therefore became lord of Glamorgan, and henceforth his territorial ambitions, and possibly a hope that one day he might see himself earl of Gloucester, kept him faithfully on the king's side. Edward clearly found him likeable, but there is no suggestion that the relationship was homosexual or even in any sense

[1] The text is in E. Pole Stuart in *E.H.R.*, XLI (1926), 412–15; cf. *Rymer*, II, 426–8 and *Baker*, 10.
[2] J. Conway Davies, *op. cit.* 90 ff.; Tout, *Place*, 15.

passionate – Despenser could be very useful to Edward, and Edward was essential to a Despenser with such overweening ambitions. Despenser, of course, was still the king's chamberlain – he proceeded to make the most of it.

When Despenser obtained Glamorgan, he had two rivals – Hugh Daudley who had married the second Gloucester sister, who was also Gaveston's widow, and Roger Damory, who was married to the youngest sister. Daudley received Newport and Netherwest, while Damory received the castle of Usk and lands in the Usk valley. Although this meant that Despenser had the best of these bargains he was still far from satisfied. In a complicated situation, Damory had the support of Pembroke, Daudley was a staunch Lancastrian, and the younger Despenser was now an ardent curialist. Despenser first manoeuvred Daudley out of Newport in exchange for estates elsewhere in England. He next obtained from Edward the life-grant of the castle of Drysllwyn and the land of Cantrev Mawr to the west of his Glamorgan lordships, and he completed his first series of aggressions by acquiring the Isle of Lundy which gave him command of the Bristol Channel. He now cast envious eyes on the peninsula of Gower, and its town and castle of Swansea. If he could acquire these, he would have a compact Despenser territorial base, stretching from the river Usk to the river Loughor. It so happened that at this time Sir William de Braose, the lord of Gower, was the impoverished last of his line. He was already trying to bargain with surrounding Lords Marcher for a cash sale when he died, leaving behind him a daughter who was married to Sir John Mowbray. Mowbray promptly seized Gower and Swansea in accordance with the 'custom of the March', and Despenser, who was a shrewd lawyer, saw his opportunity. He submitted to Edward that Mowbray's action had needed a royal licence, for which Mowbray had not even asked, and he persuaded the king to declare that Gower had escheated to the crown. Despenser was quoting English law as opposed to Marcher custom, and the other Lords Marcher were loud in their protests. The 'Middle Party' was about to split on the rocks of Despenser greed. Hereford, Despenser's near neighbour, asked Lancaster for help and advice, and an alliance quickly took shape between Despenser's two brothers-

in-law, Mowbray, Hereford, the two Mortimers, who were both
Marchers, and many native Welshmen who hated the younger
Despenser for his ruthless execution of Llewelyn Bren.[1] Their
avowed aim was to curb the new lord of Glamorgan, and to
drive both Despensers from office and fatherland. Pembroke
and Arundel stood by the king, and Lancaster, although supporting the Lords Marcher (he was himself lord of Kidwelly in
Carmarthenshire), was reluctant to take action until he was more
certain of success. Civil war in south Wales was about to break
out.[2]

Edward, in support of Despenser, moved west to Gloucester
with his armed forces, and ordered Hereford and the other
Lords Marcher to keep the peace. It was a generous but fruitless move. The Marchers were determined to enforce their
rights, and to ruin the Despensers. Hereford wrote to the king
demanding a parliament to discuss the whole affair, and the
committal of the younger Despenser in the meantime to the
custody of Lancaster. It was a fantastic request, and an unjust
slight on Despenser's honour. Edward's reply was very much to
the point – Hereford had been one of those who had confirmed
Despenser in his office as chamberlain, and Despenser was quite
ready to answer any complaints in a duly constituted parliament; there was no need for custody, and the earl should come
to the king and state his grievances in an orderly fashion. The
Marchers, however, were now impatient of debate and compromise. Early in May, they took the law into their own violent
hands and ravaged Despenser's Glamorgan.

It was at this point that Lancaster realized that he had more
to do than merely to give advice. On 24 May 1321, he called a
meeting in the chapter house of the Pontefract priory at which
he and the northern barons sealed a league for mutual aid and
defence. It was followed by a second meeting summoned to
Sherburn-in-Elmet some eight miles farther north, which was
attended by the archbishop of York, the northern bishops, the

[1] *Bridlington*, 67–8; Tout, *Place*, 125; J. Conway Davies, *op. cit.* 31–2,
cf. *supra* p. 91.
[2] W. H. Stevenson in *E.H.R.*, XII (1897), 755–61; J. Conway Davies,
The Despenser War in Glamorgan in *T.R.H.S.* (3rd ser;), IX (1915), 21–64;
Flores Hist. III, 344–5.

earl of Hereford and the two Mortimers. They met in the parish church, and drew up a long list of their grievances against the two Despensers and the king. The clergy were less co-operative than Lancaster can have hoped – they advised that the grievances should be put before the next parliament in the usual way. Nevertheless, the meeting at Sherburn-in-Elmet on 28 June sealed an indenture which marked 'the formal union of Lancaster and the barons of the Welsh march', and, there-fore, 'the break-up of the Middle Party was complete'.

Thanks to the greed of the younger Despenser, Edward was faced with a resurgent Lancaster, now the acknowledged leader of an armed rising which included the Lords Marcher and most of the midland baronage. The lords of Northumberland were not yet committed – they had reservations about a Lancaster whom they suspected of negotiating with Scots. Pembroke, throughout these months of crisis and civil war, was constantly attempting to mediate, but the chronicles record that he was secretly against the younger Despenser. Although he deplored the illegalities of the Lords Marcher, he thought it wise to advise the king that the Despensers should be dismissed, but he certainly could not have approved of the way in which his arch-enemy Lancaster had been calling meetings as though he were a king summoning his subjects to parliaments.[1]

The confederate barons, having completed their devastations in south Wales, now marched towards London with their armed retainers. Parliament was to meet at Westminster in July 1321, and the barons prepared to overawe it by occupying the approaches to London. Hereford had his men at Holborn, the Mortimers were at Clerkenwell, Daudley was at St Bartholo-mew's, and Damory was at the Temple – it was an impressive exercise in military pressure which also separated the royal court at Westminster from the royal fortress at the Tower.

The parliament was presented with a treatise which again expounded Lancaster's pet theory of the right of the hereditary

<hr/>

[1] *Baker*, 11; *Murimuth*, 33; For varying views on Lancaster's private parliaments, see *Stubbs Chronicles*, II, pp. lxxxvii–lxxxviii; Tout, *Place*, 129; M. V. Clarke, *Medieval Representation and Consent* (London, 1936), 163 and 242; B. Wilkinson in *E.H.R.*, LXIII (1948), 1–28; and J. Conway Davies, *op. cit.* 478–90; *Maddicott*, 269–79.

Steward of England to advise the king on every detail of administration, and to control his counsellors.[1] Edward tried delaying tactics, but he was at the mercy of overwhelming forces. The barons were ready for desperate measures – 'he should hear their complaints or they would utterly renounce their homage and set up another ruler'. It was a grave if traitorous threat, but Pembroke – and even Isabella – advised the king to bow to it. Unwillingly, Edward agreed to the baron's terms – both the Despensers were arraigned in a formidable list of misdemeanours, 'and there was no one to defend either father or son, and no one to speak for them against the barons'.[2] On 19 August 1321, judgment was pronounced in Westminster Hall – both Despensers were condemned to perpetual exile and to disinheritance. The chroniclers approved of the exile but questioned the justice of the disinheritance, and indeed its wisdom – it provided an excuse for future recrimination and retribution.[3] The parliament closed with the usual issue of pardons to the barons concerned.

The elder Despenser accepted his sentence with reasonable grace, and Edward escorted him with honour to his port of departure at Harwich. The younger Despenser was less amenable; he 'became a sea-monster'. In other words, with the aid of the men and ships of the Cinque Ports, he took to profitable piracy in the Channel – he captured one of the great Genoese galleys which later cost Edward III some 8,000 marks in compensation.[4]

During the ascendancy of Pembroke and the 'Middle Party', Edward had displayed an intelligence and a devotion to royal duties which earned him the appreciation of at least one observer. In 1320, Thomas Cobham, bishop of Worcester, noted in his register that he was delighted that the king was rising early in the morning to face his duties, co-operating pleasantly with his advisers both clerical and lay, and making useful

[1] M. V. Clarke, op. cit. 242; L. W. Vernon Harcourt, op. cit. 164–7; Ann. Paul., 293.
[2] Vita, 112–15; Tout, Place, 130–1.
[3] Vita, 115.
[4] Vita, 115; Rymer, II, 941.

contributions to debate.[1] And Edward's prowess in diplomatic negotiations has already been noticed. All in all, by the autumn of 1321, Edward of Caernarvon had matured into a formidable personality. He was still the injured friend of Gaveston; he had again had to submit to baronial fetters, he had again had to sacrifice intimate friends – but he had not yet despaired of a final reckoning with all those who had so persistently infringed his regality. The days of Pembroke's compromises were numbered.

[1] E. H. Pearce, *Register of Thomas de Cobham*, Worcester Hist. Soc. (Worcester, 1930), 97–8. The praise is somewhat qualified by the comment 'contrary to his wont'.

Chapter 10

LEEDS
AND
BOROUGHBRIDGE

The proceedings of the Westminster parliament of 1321 enraged Edward, and he had no intention of allowing its edicts to stand. For the moment he was compelled to acquiesce, but not to approve – he was watching anxiously for the moment when he could reinstate his friends, and still hoping to avenge his murdered Gaveston. It is ironical that the opportunity for very wholesale vengeance came quickly enough through one of the leaders of the 'Middle Party' of compromise – Bartholomew lord Badlesmere.

Badlesmere was originally a knight of the shire of Kent, holding his land from the archbishop of Canterbury. He had become a knight of the earl of Gloucester, and through him found a patron in the earl of Hereford, and later a substantial administrative position at court. He first appeared as a person of some consequence when he was appointed to the embassy to the pope led by Pembroke at the end of 1316, and, although his early career was with the court, he had become a leader of the 'Middle Party'. He prospered, became warden of Bristol Castle and later constable of the royal castle at Leeds in Kent. In 1318 he was appointed steward to Edward's household, and therefore earned the bitter enmity of Lancaster. During the hegemony of the 'Middle Party' Badlesmere had had sufficient influence with Edward to secure the appointment of his nephew Henry Burghersh – not yet thirty – to the bishopric of Lincoln. But, as the Despensers' influence supervened, Badlesmere drifted into jealous opposition, and, during the Glamorgan civil wars and at the Westminster parliament of 1321, he finally broke with the Despensers and the curialists.[1] Although he obtained (and needed) the royal pardon for his share in the Despensers' exile, he did not dare to reappear as royal steward, yet his tenure of that office precluded any reconciliation with Lancaster. His position, therefore, at the end of the year 1321 was both isolated and precarious.

On 13 October 1321, Queen Isabella happened to be journeying to Canterbury, and, on her way, she found it advisable to ask for a night's hospitality at Leeds Castle near Maidstone. Badlesmere was absent, but his wife and his kinsman, Bartholomew Burghersh, were in residence. Unaccountably, Lady Badlesmere refused to admit the queen, on the absurd grounds that she could admit no one without her husband's permission. The queen in fury found quarters in the neighbouring priory, and ordered her small escort to force the castle gates. The attack was a failure, and six of her entourage were killed. Isabella lost no time in urging her husband to deal with this appalling insult to monarchy – and Edward was more than ready to help. Summoning the local levies, Edward also hired professional soldiery and rapidly assembled a sizeable army, including a detachment of Londoners, to mount a full-scale siege of the great moated castle. The justness of Edward's case is attested by the fact that he was quickly joined by six earls – Pembroke, Surrey, Arundel, Richmond, and his young half-brothers the earls of Norfolk and of Kent. In just over a week, Leeds Castle surrendered. Lady Badlesmere was sent prisoner to Dover Castle, Burghersh to the Tower, and thirteen of the garrison were hanged forthwith.[2]

Meanwhile, Badlesmere himself had been canvassing for baronial support against the king without much success. Lancaster, of course, he could not approach, but he succeeded in persuading Hereford and the Mortimers to help, and they brought their joint forces to a muster at Kingston-upon-

[1] Tout, *Place*, 122, 132–4; *Genesis*, I, 120–1; J. Conway Davies, *op. cit.* 42, 482.

[2] *Ann. Paul.*, 298–9; *Trokelowe*, 110–11; *Baker*, 11–12; *Vita*, 116; *Murimuth*, 35; *Flores Hist.*, III, 199–200. The magnificent castle still survives just off the main road from London to Canterbury near Maidstone.

Thames only to hear that Leeds Castle had already fallen. They dispersed to the west, while Lancaster, although still remaining aloof, began to muster his own private army in the north. Edward realized that at last the moment had come to strike with a vengeance – he first took his forces to the west in pursuit of the Lords Marcher.

Towards the end of the year 1321, it was clear that a major civil war was about to break out. It was to be, in the words of a distinguished modern historian, 'a duel to the death between the royal cousins, and a conflict of principle between monarchy under control and a monarchy free and unfettered.'[1] In November, Lancaster again summoned one of his personal unofficial parliaments – this time to Doncaster. A damning document has survived – sometimes called the Doncaster Petition[2] – in which Lancaster and his friends listed the usual complaints against the king, but which definitely threatened armed rebellion if their grievances were not settled. On his side, Edward was now ready to meet this traitorous challenge with well-placed and ample forces, and the approval of the rest of the magnates. He spent Christmas at Cirencester, and had already persuaded the convocation of Canterbury, under the presidency of his old friend Archbishop Reynolds, to declare the sentences against the Despensers invalid. In the New Year, he continued his pursuit of the Marchers up the Severn valley. In mid-January 1322, both the Despensers arrived back from their short exile,[3] and Edward had additional encouragement when one of his oldest household officials, Sir Gruffydd Llwyd, at this opportune moment mounted a revolt of the Welsh of Snowdonia against the hated Mortimers.[4] The Lords Marcher were on the west bank of the Severn, and successfully held all the bridges until Edward was able to cross from the east bank at Shrewsbury. The rebels now lost their nerve. They were threatened in their rear by Llwyd and his Welsh mountaineers, and they had no assistance from Lancaster. The Mortimers

[1] H. Johnstone in *C.M.H.*, VII, 424.
[2] See G. L. Haskins in *E.H.R.*, LIII (1938), 478–85; *Maddicott*, 295–301.
[3] *Rymer*, II, 471; *Ann Paul.*, 301.
[4] See J. G. Edwards in *E.H.R.*, XXX (1915), 589–601; Tout, *Chapters*, II, 172 and 209.

tamely and abjectly surrendered while Hereford, Mowbray, Damory and a few more escaped to seek Lancaster sulking at Pontefract. The Mortimers were sent prisoners to the Tower, and Daudley and Berkeley to Wallingford Castle.[1] Edward returned south taking over the greater Marcher castles on the way including Hereford, where he berated the bishop, Adam of Orleton, for his support of rebellion, and the fateful castle of Berkeley near Bristol. The first passages of the royal duel were decidedly in Edward's favour.

The next stage found Edward concentrating his forces at Coventry ready to march north against a Lancaster who was now openly plotting treason. In December 1321 Lancaster had sent his agents to Sir James Douglas, in February 1322 he had sent Mowbray and Clifford to the earl of Moray, and later a draft of a treaty was discovered by which Bruce and Lancaster were pledged to mutual aid against their enemies. One of the chroniclers casually refers to 'forged documents', but the evidence for Lancaster's treason taken as a whole is convincing.[2] From Bruce's point of view, civil war in England was to his advantage, and it is an additional charge against Lancaster that, while Bruce's men were again savagely raiding Northumberland Durham and north Yorkshire, he, with his ample forces at Pontefract, did nothing to stop them. Sir Andrew Harclay, warden of Carlisle, came hot-foot to Edward to advise him of the Scottish danger, and to ask for instructions. He was told to hold his men in readiness to attack the English rebels before replying to Bruce's new invasions.

There are some obscurities about the next moves on both sides. The established facts are that hostilities began with Lancaster's forces inexplicably wasting three weeks in an unsuccessful siege of the royal castle of Tickhill just south of Doncaster. They then more sensibly marched south – some sixty miles to Burton-on-Trent in order to bar Edward's way north. Unfortunately for the Lancastrians, Edward's forces

[1] *Vita*, 119; G. L. Haskins in *Speculum*, XIV (1939), 78; *Flores Hist.*, III, 201.

[2] *Trokelowe*, 118–20; *Ann. Paul.*, 302; *Rymer*, II, 463, 472; *Genesis*, I, 124; *C.D.S.*, III, No. 764. Lancaster's latest biographer writes 'the comulative evidence for Lancaster's collaboration with the Scots is very strong' – *Maddicott*, 302.

found a suitable ford higher up the Trent, made the crossing, and so forced the Lancastrians into panicky retreat. They retired seventy-five miles north to their central stronghold at Pontefract with the royal forces in close pursuit. The Lancastrian castle of Tutbury was taken by Edward on the way, and there Damory was captured, mortally wounded. The Lancastrians retreated farther north, perhaps in the hope of finding the promised help from Bruce – they were grievously disappointed. As they approached the long narrow bridge over the river Ure at Boroughbridge, north-west of York, they were met by Sir Andrew Harclay and his levies from Cumberland and West-morland in occupation of the north end of the bridge. The baronial rebels were now cut off from Bruce, and foolishly they divided forces. Hereford and Clifford dismounted and tried to force the bridge by direct assault, while Lancaster and his mounted men-at-arms attempted to cross the Ure by a near-by ford and take Harclay in the flank. Harclay had learned in the Scottish wars the value of the dismounted 'schiltrom', and he now deployed his men in this formation and supported them with concentrated archery on their flanks. The direct attack on the bridge petered out when Hereford died horribly, speared from below through a gap in the planks of the bridge, and Clifford was severely wounded. Meanwhile, Harclay's long-bows were decimating Lancaster's cavalry before they could reach the ford. The situation of the rebels was desperate, and Lancaster asked for a truce until the following morning. The request was granted but during the night most of Hereford's men deserted, and Lancaster realized bitterly that his favourite knight from Lancashire – Sir Robert Holland – had no intention of coming to his aid.[1] To complete his discomfiture, at day-break of 17 March 1322, the sheriff of York arrived with royalist reinforcements from the south – the Lancastrians were hopelessly trapped, and the battle of Boroughbridge ended in their total and ignominious surrender. Lancaster, Clifford, Mowbray and the other rebels were Harclay's prisoners.[2]

[1] Tout, *Chapters*, II, 185–7; J. Conway Davies, *op. cit.* 503–4; *Vita*, 122–3.
[2] See T. F. Tout in *E.H.R.*, XIX (1904), 711–15; *Lanercost*, 234; *Vita*, 121–4; J. E. Morris in *Trans. Cumberland and Westmorland Archl. Assoc.* (New Series), III, 307 ff.

This strange battle was between Englishmen, and it has achieved some fame because it was the first time that English soldiers used the tactics which later won the battles of Crécy and Agincourt. In future, dismounted men-at-arms protected by long-bow archers were to be the English answer to foreign numerical superiority. Boroughbridge was, too, a victory for brilliant strategy. If the tactics of this battle redound to the credit of Harclay, Edward can claim some credit for its strategy. In medieval warfare generalship was of less account than individual prowess, but, if Edward must be blamed for Bannockburn, he must equally be praised for Boroughbridge.

Harclay's prisoners were immediately sent south to Pontefract where Edward awaited them. A trial was staged in the great hall of Lancaster's favourite castle. Seven earls and many great barons were present under the presidency of the king himself. It was not a legal trial; Lancaster was not permitted to speak in his own defence, and there was no one willing to speak for him. But a long list of Lancaster's offences was read out, and his peers were asked to pass judgment on him. There could be only one verdict – he was condemned to death as a rebel and as a traitor, and only his royal blood saved him from the worst penalties – he was granted the short shrift of decapitation. On 22 March 1322, on a small hill outside his own castle walls, Thomas earl of Lancaster, dressed as a penitent and mounted on 'a sorry nag', was escorted through the jeers and snowballing of the surrounding mob to his doom. His head was inexpertly hacked from his body, and his remains were buried before the high altar of Pontefract priory.[1] Proscription of the other rebels followed mercilessly; Clifford and Mowbray were hanged at York, Badlesmere was hanged at Canterbury and over twenty more rebels paid with their lives for Lancaster's treason. The royal duel was over – Edward had won.

Thomas, earl of Lancaster, was a puzzling and unlikeable character even to his contemporaries. Born to great possessions, married to a great heiress, a close relative of kings and queens, he had everything in his favour; yet his career had no glimmer

[1] *Trokelowe*, 112–24; *Flores Hist.*, III, 205–7; G. L. Haskins in *Speculum*, XIV (1939), 73–81; *Ann. Paul.*, 302–3; *Rymer*, II, 478; *Vita*, 125–6. The best chronicler account of the battle is undoubtedly in *Brut*, I, 219–24.

of greatness, no suggestion of charm, no example of loyalty to his king or even of devotion to his own best interests. He was both vicious and idle, and he died without a friend. It is a sad commentary on vulgar credulity that the absentee from Bannockburn, the deserter of his own allies, the traitor to his king, was soon hailed as a saint by the populace.[1] In a recent detailed study of Thomas of Lancaster's career a modern historian has made a learned attempt to justify that canonisation. He has compared Lancaster to Simon de Montfort, he has lauded his motives for and his loyalty to the Ordinances, and yet in the end he has had to admit that Lancaster was 'a rapacious, grasping and cruel landlord', that, even if he was 'more than customarily devout', he was nevertheless a lecher and guilty of a 'violent feuding which in its brutality and violence was unusual even by fourteenth-century standards', that in his dealing with the Scots 'his name was stained with treachery', that he 'showed few signs of political ability', and that perhaps ill-health may have been the only explanation of his 'tragic failure'.[2]

In any event the murderer of Gaveston could have expected no mercy from Edward of Caernarvon – he deserved none, and he found none.

[1] *Higden,* VIII, 314; *Flores Hist.,* III, 206–7.
[2] *Maddicott,* 318–34.

Chapter 11

TRIUMPH
AND
DISASTER

A few weeks after Edward's rough justice had dealt with the Lancastrian leaders, a full parliament was summoned to York. In the story of the evolution of the English parliamentary system, this parliament of May 1322 has gained a distinguished place for two reasons. First, it was the first English parliament to include representatives from Wales – there were forty-eight of the 'more discreet, more legally-minded and more substantial' Welsh from north and south Wales outside the king's principality.[1] Second, in repealing the Ordinances of 1311, and establishing Edward's full 'regality' once again, a phrase was used which was to have far more significance for later Whig lawyers than it had for medieval barons. It decided that 'matters which are to be established for the estate of our lord the king . . . and for the estate of the realm and of the people, shall be treated, accorded and established in parliament, by our lord the king and by the assent of the prelates, earls, and barons, *and the commonalty of the realm*; according as it hath been heretofore accustomed.'[2] Much ink has flowed since in disputed interpretations of the italicized words, and in varying opinions as to their real significance. To Edward and his contemporaries, there was no new doctrine here – the phrase immediately following makes that specifically clear, and the principle that 'what concerns all must be approved by all' had long been accepted. Moreover, the previous paragraph had re-emphasized the monarchical

[1] Tout, *Place*, 136–7; *Rymer*, II, 484.
[2] *Stats.*, I, 189; Stephenson and Marcham, *op. cit.* 204–5.

doctrine that the king's regality could not be encroached by 'any power or authority whatsoever'. The men of 1322 were concerned with parliament as a court of justice rather than as a stronghold of democracy – they looked to parliament to punish the defeated and reward the victorious. Nevertheless, it is not to the discredit of Edward, or of the Despensers, that future constitutional experts should be able to point to this clause of their York Statute as justifying the claim that all important legislation needed the co-operation of the commons in a full parliament.[1]

The detailed proceedings of this 1322 parliament at York are unfortunately missing, but there exists one interesting document[2] which was circulated to its members as a kind of agenda to save time – and as a result the commons were only in attendance for less than three weeks, while the magnates continued business for a further six weeks. It was obviously a most business-like assembly. An earldom and supporting finances were approved for Harclay, the victor of Boroughbridge – he was created earl of Carlisle. The elder Despenser became earl of Winchester, and, surprisingly, his son was *not* rewarded with the earldom of Gloucester. But if Edward's unusual moderation suggested that an earldom for his new favourite minister might be going too far, he took good care to compensate him with overwhelming booty and bounty. The confiscated manors and castles of the defeated Lords Marcher gave the younger Despenser control of all south Wales, saving of course the royal lands of the Principality, besides many rich estates in many parts of England. This mood of generosity mixed with caution even seems to have infected the younger Despenser himself – under his auspices, the 1322 parliament re-issued some of the repealed Ordinances of 1311 as 'establishments' aimed at protecting the liberties of subjects and reforming the machinery of administration. There were 'establishments' dealing with the church, prises, the forests, and the excessive authority of steward and

[1] M. V. Clarke, *Medieval Representation, op. cit.* 139 and 154 ff.; G. T. Lapsley in *E.H.R.*, XXVIII (1913), 118–24 and *E.H.R.*, LVI (1941), 22–51, 411–46; J. Conway Davies, *op. cit.* 512–18; J. R. Strayer in *A.H.R..* XLVII (1941), 1–23; G. L. Haskins in *E.H.R.*, LII (1937), 74–7; B. Wilkinson in *Speculum*, LIX (1944), 445–70.

[2] J. Conway Davies, *op. cit.* 582–3.

marshal, while the Ordinances dealing with outlawry and with merchants were reissued *verbatim*. As a modern historian has ruefully observed, 'few seemed to realize the magnanimity of the king in adopting the good reforms of his bitterest enemies'.[1] Although the 1322 parliament of York released the king from all baronial interference, Edward and his personal officials were clearly not averse to sensible and agreed reforms. Its statutes included the good works of the 1316 parliament at Lincoln, of the 1318 parliament at York, as well as the most sensible of the Ordinances of 1311, and, while vehemently rejecting any restrictions on the king's regality, it gave permanent approval to what had hitherto been an occasional concession – the right of the 'community' to be consulted on fundamental matters which clearly concerned it. On the whole, the 1322 parliament of York deserved its subsequent fame, and Edward II and the younger Despenser can deservedly share the credit.

There was now time and opportunity to turn to the problems of the north. The two-year truce with Bruce expired in the summer of 1322. At the beginning of July, Bruce himself led a lightning raid on the west which harried as far south as Preston. It was decided that yet another invasion of Scotland must be undertaken with speed, and Edward summoned his forces to Newcastle; in August they advanced to the Border. The Scots in Berwick stubbornly held out, and Edward therefore by-passed them and proceeded to ravage the Lothians in pursuit of Bruce's main army. Holyrood Abbey was sacked, but Bruce held to his settled policy of avoiding pitched battles and retired north of the Forth. He left behind him a 'scorched earth', which provided Edward with neither food nor fighting. Barbour tells the story of the earl of Surrey who, on finding only one lame cow in all the Lothians, remarked that it was 'the dearest beef that ever I saw: surely it has cost a thousand pounds and more'.[2] At Melrose they were attacked by the Douglas in a 'hit and run' skirmish, but the English forces were able to continue their retreat. Bruce now chose the right moment for a brilliant move –

[1] *Rot. Parl.*, I, 456–7 App. no. 35; Tout, *Place*, 136–7. The quotation is from J. Conway Davies, *op. cit.* 492–4.

[2] Barbour, *Bruce*, 330; *Lanercost*, 239.

12 Berkeley Castle (near Bristol)

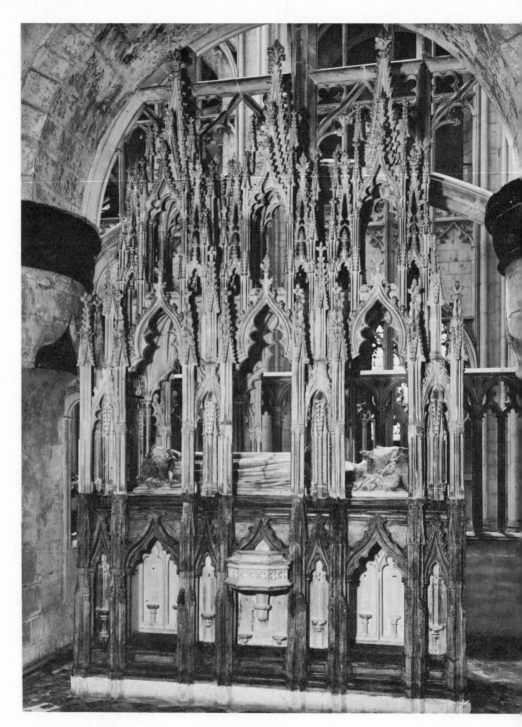

13 Edward II's tomb, Gloucester

he took a large force over the Solway border and up the Eden valley to attack Edward's retreating forces in the flank or rear. When Bruce reached Northallerton in north Yorkshire, Edward and his queen were only fifteen miles away at the abbey of Rievaulx, ignorant of danger. On 14 October 1322, Bruce, with Douglas and Moray, surprised part of Edward's army under the Breton earl of Richmond at Old Byland, and routed it. Richmond, Sir Ralph Cobham, Henry de Sully, butler of France, and many more were taken prisoner, and Edward himself only just managed to escape to Bridlington, and, by very roundabout tracks, to the safety of York's walls with the Scots in close pursuit right up to the city gates, while Isabella escaped from Tynemouth by a very rough sea. It was a sorry end to what proved to be Edward's last campaign against the Scots, and once again he had had to abandon his treasure, baggage, and even his harness and the privy seal. Bruce left him in York, and, before turning back to Scotland, made a quick and saucy dash eastwards to levy blackmail from Beverley only ten miles from Hull. Richmond was held captive by Bruce for two years, but Sully, and one or two more French friends of Edward, were released immediately without ransom – Bruce was hoping that the 'auld alliance' might soon be in action again.[1]

The near-total disaster at Old Byland had left the north once again at the marauder's mercy, and by this time it is not surprising that many northerners had decided that they had had more than enough of raid and counter-raid – not a few decided to make shift for themselves. The monks of Bridlington, for example,[2] shipped their valuables south of the Humber and opened up direct negotiations with the Scots, and an old protégé of Edward's queen, Louis de Beaumont, bishop of Durham, did likewise. But the defection which must have cut Edward to the quick was that of Andrew Harclay, the new earl of Carlisle and warden of the northern Marches. He and his men had been in the action at Old Byland, and afterwards he dismissed his troops and followed Bruce to Lochmaben in

---

[1] *Scalacronica*, 149–50; Barbour, *Bruce*, 128–34; *Flores Hist.*, III, 260; *Trokelowe*, 125–6;

[2] *Bridlington*, 81.

Dumfriesshire, where he entered into direct and traitorous negotiations with the Scottish king. They agreed that a permanent peace should be arranged on the basis that Bruce would be recognized as King Robert I of Scotland, and that a committee of six Scottish and six English lords would be empowered to work out detailed terms. Within a year, Bruce would pay about £27,000 in return for the renunciation of England's claim to suzerainty, and peace would be cemented by a marriage between Bruce's heir and any member of England's royal family whom Edward might choose. A damning clause in the agreement provided for the protection of Harclay's estates if ever again Bruce's forces had to cross the Border.[1] On the face of it, the violent reactions of Edward and the Despensers seem unjustified. Harclay was facing facts as the monks of Bridlington had done, and taking sensible action. But bargaining for private immunity is not the concomitant of honest diplomacy, and in any event Harclay's action was completely 'ultra vires', and an insult to his king and his peers. It is not really surprising that when Edward and the Despensers heard of these transactions they were appalled, and ordered Harclay's immediate arrest. A certain 'famous' Cumberland knight, Sir Anthony Lucy, who had been an intimate friend of Harclay's, undertook the unpleasant duty. As an old friend, he was welcomed into Carlisle Castle, where Harclay was in residence. Once inside, he revealed his treachery, and forcibly arrested the earl. A correct but hasty judicial trial followed, and Harclay was inevitably condemned to death as a traitor. On 3 March 1323, the earl of Carlisle bravely suffered sentence on the Carlisle gallows. His head was sent to London, and, to the plaudits of the mayor and citizens, it was posted above London Bridge.

It is a tragic episode, and it illustrates the savagery of the times. Harclay's negotiations with Bruce were clearly traitorous and he must have known the risks he ran, but there is no warranty for the report in the Brut chronicle which also blames him for treachery at Old Byland. His motives seem to have been reasonable and comprehensible; his actions seem to have been those of a man who had risen too quickly, and who, in spite of

---

[1] *Proc. Soc. Antiq. Scot.*, III (1897–60), 458–61; J. E. Morris in *Trans. Cumberland and Westmorland Archl. Soc.* New Series, III (1903), 307 ff.

real merits as a soldier, hazarded, and lost, everything by thinking that he could therefore negotiate with kings on behalf of kings. The fourteenth-century earl of Carlisle is a classic example in English history of the ancient Greek sin of 'hubris'. And the ironic sequel to so sad a story is that when peace with Scotland eventually came (in 1328), its terms closely resembled the projected arrangements of Harclay and Bruce at Lochmaben, save that the price which Bruce was ultimately willing to pay was less.[1]

Meanwhile, official negotiations for peace with Bruce had been going on with Pembroke and the younger Despenser as heads of the English commission. The stumbling block was the persistent refusal of England to recognize Bruce's royal title, and negotiations ended merely with a thirteen-years' truce confirmed at Bishopthorpe just outside York on 30 May 1323.[2] Edward and the Despensers could claim that at least they had achieved peace for a considerable period without sacrificing the hereditary claims of the English crown, and without going back on their obligations to the legitimate Scottish royal line of the Balliols. In this sense Edward had in fact 'kept faith' with his father.

In spite of the disaster near Rievaulx and the defection of Harclay, the prospects for Edward and the Despensers in the summer of the year 1323 must have seemed bright. Thomas of Lancaster, Humphrey of Hereford and Guy of Warwick were dead, the Mortimers were in the Tower, Surrey and Arundel were of little account, Richmond was a prisoner in Scotland, and Norfolk and Kent were too young to be yet in the reckoning. As for possible rivals, the heir to Lancaster was his brother Henry, an elderly moderate who seemed to be without ambitions and who threatened no one. He was soon allowed to take over his late brother's earldom of Leicester – there was as yet nothing to fear from this quarter. Pembroke, the faithful peacemaker, seemed at this period to be tiring of affairs of state. He had recently been in France for his third marriage,

---

[1] *Rymer*, II, 509; *Trokelowe*, 126–7; *Bridlington*, 82–3; *Murimuth*, 39; *Flores Hist.*, III, 211–12; *Brut*, I, 226–7.
[2] *Rymer*, II, 520, 521, 524; *Flores Hist.*, III, 265–6; *Vita*, 132–3.

but he had returned in time to side against the Despensers in 1321. On the other hand, he had sat on the tribunal which sentenced Lancaster. Whatever the reason, it is on record that in 1323 Edward was 'aggrieved against him', and obliged him to renew a solemn pledge of personal loyalty. He had since been so far reconciled with the king that he had accompanied him in the expedition against Bruce, and had helped in the negotiations leading to the thirteen-years' truce. But Pembroke was never a threat to the throne. Edward could give both the Despensers a free hand in the confidence that there appeared to be no opposition left – they were not slow to make the most of it.[1]

As chamberlain, the younger Despenser was now instrumental in initiating and carrying through a series of administrative reforms of some importance. He had the goodwill of the king, he had the long and wide experience of his father and he had some very able assistance from Walter Stapledon, bishop of Exeter, William Melton, archbishop of York, and Robert Baldock, keeper of the privy seal, and in 1323 the chancellor.

Throughout the reign of Edward II, there were persistent attempts of the baronage to control the monarchy by obtaining control of those royal household offices which were so inextricably involved with offices of state, and to ensure that the king's finances were controlled by such state departments as the exchequer and the chancery. The younger Despenser had been an enthusiastic Ordainer, and the reforms carried out between 1323 and 1326 under his aegis are a tribute to his intelligence and his independence of thought.

There were three series of enactments for which the younger Despenser, Stapledon (and later Melton) and Baldock were chiefly responsible – the Cowick Ordinances of 1323, the Westminster Ordinances of 1324 and 1326, and the Kenilworth Ordinance of 1326. They reorganized the exchequer, the wardrobe and the vitally important overseas trade, and many of their regulations were continued in the following reign. There was only one development with which Edward himself was

[1] Tout, *Place*, 142 ff.; Tout, *Chapters*, II, 314–60; Tout, *The English Civil Service in the Fourteenth Century* (Manchester, 1916), *passim*.

closely concerned – the Despensers' answer to control by committees of barons, and submissions to parliaments, was the new power centred in the royal 'chamber'.[1] The younger Despenser expanded his own office of chamberlain so that it could acquire lands and revenues outside the control of the exchequer, issue writs and letters in spite of the established rights of the chancery, and use its own 'secret seal' to help the king to 'live of his own' without interference and in reasonable comfort. The Kenilworth Ordinance altered the 'staple' system of controlling trade, and therefore profoundly affected the economics of the whole realm. Hitherto the staple – the places through which foreign trade was compelled to go – had been established at Antwerp, Bruges and more recently at St Omer. Despenser, perhaps in a bid for popularity with the English merchants at a time when he was beginning to need it, decreed on 1 May 1326 that the staple should henceforth be shared between nine English, two Welsh and three Irish towns, and it was to apply to wool, woolfells and leather. Whether Edward himself was very much personally concerned with such administrative detail is doubtful, but the reforms of the Despenser period have received such lengthy praise from so many historians of administration and economics that at least Edward deserves some credit for appointing and supporting the man most responsible.

However posterity has rated the Despensers, they rated themselves very highly, and Edward, as usual, was more than generous to those who served him. Modern scholars have been able to measure the extent of the appetite of the younger Despenser, and there were some of his contemporaries who alleged that his father was even more grasping.[2] At the beginning of September 1324 the chamberlain's deposits with Florentine bankers totalled £6,000 and within two years he had deposited a further £5,735, and this was only a fraction of his total resources. Most of his wealth came from his vast estates – they soon covered most of the Clare inheritance, many English manors from lords now wholly on Bruce's side, a fat share in the

---

[1] Tout, *Place*, 152, 176–81 and 220 ff.; *C.M.H.*, VII, 431; Tout, *Chapters*, 211; E. Power, *The Wool Trade* (Oxford, 1941), *passim*.

[2] E. B. Fryde in *Econ. Hist. Rev.* 2nd ser., III (1951), 344–62; Tout, *Place*, 124 ff.; J. Conway Davies, *op. cit.* 91–5, 97–8, 102–3.

confiscations of Templar property, and rich portions from the proscribed Lancastrians. The efficiency of the Despensers has never been questioned, but their avarice was monumental – the combination resulted in an unpopularity with all classes which finally left both father and son with only one friend – Edward. Moreover, the younger Despenser, wise in so many ways, committed the fatal folly of antagonizing Queen Isabella. A period which had begun in rosy optimism was to end in disaster.

But what logicians call the 'proximate cause' of disaster was a comparatively unimportant complication in foreign affairs, which soon reached the dimensions of international crisis and national rebellion. Relations with France in the fourteenth century were bound up with the royal involvements in the south-west of France – and to a much lesser extent in Ponthieu – with the Franco–Scottish alliance, with commercial rivalries in the Low Countries, and with the struggle for control of the Narrow Seas. Edward's marriage to Isabella of France had been, as a diplomatic move, a resounding success; the Scots had had very little encouragement from France, and it was service in Edward's armies that adventuring French knights seemed to prefer. The only recurring trouble was the necessity for swearing fealty. The fact that a sovereign also had to be a vassal was almost certain to result in awkward complications, and it was un-fortunate that, during Edward's reign, there were successively four kings of France. To England, Gascony 'yielded a revenue greater than that of the English crown', and the wine merchants and wine makers of this rich province owed neither affection nor loyalty to the kings in Paris.[1] To France, Gascony was a continuing challenge – by geography and largely by race it was destined one day to cease to be English. The seeds of what the history books call The Hundred Years War had been sown early, and under Edward II they first began to sprout.

Charles IV, the third son of Edward's father-in-law Philip IV, became king of France in 1322. In September of the follow-ing year, when the Lancastrians had been crushed and when a truce had been arranged between England and Scotland,

[1] Gascons regarded Frenchmen as foreigners down to at least the late fifteenth century.

Charles IV politely reminded Edward that he owed him fealty. He invited Edward to meet him at Amiens by Easter of 1324 – a date subsequently extended to 1 July. Meanwhile, trouble had arisen on the Gascon borders over Saint Sardos[1], a priory in the Agenais district which belonged to the Benedictines of French Sarlat farther north. The French had decided that Saint Sardos was an excellent place for a 'bastide' – a new fortified town. In November 1323 work was about to begin when, on hearing of it, Sir Ralph Basset, the English seneschal of Gascony, attacked Saint Sardos and hanged a French serjeant on a make-shift gallows displaying the arms of France. Basset had an accomplice in Raymond Bernard, lord of Montpezat, and the French king, having accepted Edward's protestations that he had known nothing of the outrage, summoned both marauders to judgment at Toulouse in January 1324. The Gascons defaulted, and Charles IV quite legitimately declared them banished and their estates forfeit. The young earl of Kent was sent as the head of an embassy to Paris which did nothing to improve matters. It was made to appear that Edward was not only condoning the Saint Sardos outrage but refusing the homage which he clearly owed to Charles. Gascony and Ponthieu were declared confiscate, and hostilities broke out. Kent was appointed to command the somewhat meagre English forces in Gascony, and, when Charles of Valois invaded Edward's duchy in August 1324, Kent retreated to the castle of La Réole on the River Garonne some thirty miles up-stream from Bordeaux. On 22 September 1324, Kent capitulated, and agreed to a six months' truce.

Edward and the Despensers were both furious and dismayed. Kent's ineptitude had been disastrous, yet they were reluctant and quite unprepared, to enter upon a major war. Instead, after some hasty and unsuccessful attempts to raise men and commission ships, they sent yet another embassy to the French court, this time under Pembroke. This chapter of accidents was completed when Pembroke fell ill and suddenly died shortly

[1] Tout, *Place*, 191–202; E. C. Lodge, *Gascony under English Rule* (London, 1926), 71; E. Pole Stuart in *Bull. Inst. Hist. Research*, V, 171–4; P. Chaplais, *The War of Saint Sardos*, Camden, 3rd ser., LXXXVII (1954), *passim*.

after landing in France. At this critical juncture, the new pope, John XXII at Avignon, became involved – he needed peace in the west in order that the Saracen might be defeated in the east. Papal nuncios were sent to Paris, and they made the fateful suggestion that Edward's Queen Isabella, sister of Charles IV, might be able to bring the two sides together. Edward and the Despensers surprisingly agreed, and on 9 March 1325 Isabella and most of her household sailed for France. It was the prologue to a squalid tragedy which was soon to include adultery, rebellion, deposition and murder.

Chapter 12

ISABELLA

When, in March 1325, Isabella left England as ambassador-extraordinary to the court of her brother, Charles IV, she had become the dominating personality in a miscellaneous group whose sole binding agent was its hatred of the power and pride of the Despensers. How had such an unnatural development come about?

Isabella was now a mature women of twenty-nine, and she had been married to Edward for seventeen years. As a girl-wife, she had dutifully provided an heir to the throne of England, and later she had produced a second son and two daughters.[1] On her arrival in England, she was quickly made aware of the sad fact that her husband's first preference was for the society of his beloved 'Perrot'. Some of her compatriots, who had accompanied her to England after her wedding, had been understandably angry at Edward's neglect of her, and there were many English critics who had noted with disgust that many of the jewels in her dowry were soon decorating the outlandish Gascon clothes of the peacock Gaveston.[2] Yet Isabella, on the whole, had been very well treated. She was given a large and splendid household of her own with a domestic staff of nearly two hundred, and she was endowed with the revenues of the counties of Ponthieu and Montreuil, and given the honours of Wallingford and St Valéry to provide financial support.[3] It

---

[1] J. Conway Davies, *op. cit.* 105–6. Her second son was John of Eltham (b. 1316) later earl of Cornwall; her daughters were Eleanor of Woodstock (b.1318), later married to the count of Gelderland, and Joan of the Tower (b.1321), who was to be the bride of David II, king of Scotland.

[2] For Isabella's jewels and dowry see W. E. Rhodes in *E.H.R.*, XII (1897), 517–21: *Maddicott*, 131; *Ann. Paul.*, 258–62.

[3] H. Johnstone on *The Queen's Household* in Tout, *Chapters*, V, 241–50; also on *Isabella, the She-wolf of France* in *History*, new ser., XXI (1936), 208–18; Tout, *Place*, 140–1; *Rymer*, II, 569.

was true that she once had occasion to complain to her father, Philip IV of France, of Gaveston's avarice, but, after Gaveston's murder, she appears in the records chiefly in the pleasant role of peacemaker between her husband and the magnates. The 'treaty' of Leake owed something to her endeavours, and she had tried to mitigate Edward's vengeance after Boroughbridge. When a young mother of only eighteen, she had served on a peace mission to her father's court, and her obstinacy and determination were early in evidence. In 1316, when she and Edward favoured different candidates for the see of Rochester, it had been the king who had had to give way – much to the astonishment of visiting cardinals. In 1318, when she wanted her friend Louis de Beaumont made bishop of Durham, she had been able to persuade her husband to withdraw his own nominee, and she had also obtained papal support for Beaumont. Clearly she was a very forceful character.

It was after the triumph of Edward over Lancaster in 1322 that there were early whispers that the king and queen were beginning to drift apart, and, as the Despensers began to establish themselves as the real masters of England, the queen had become the focal point of a movement dedicated to the favourites' overthrow. She first found support in three ecclesiastics whom her husband, with much justification, detested. Shortly after Boroughbridge, Edward had written to Pope John XXII hoping that he could get rid of Henry Burghersh bishop of Lincoln, Adam of Orleton bishop of Hereford, and John of Droxford bishop of Bath and Wells. Burghersh was a nephew of the executed Badlesmere and therefore Edward's implacable enemy; Orleton was the protégé of the rebel Sir Roger Mortimer of Wigmore and had offended Edward by supporting his patron during the Severn campaign before the battle of Boroughbridge; Droxford was the careerist friend of both Burghersh and Orleton. These three unamiable and self-seeking clerics were soon joined by John Stratford bishop of Winchester whose appointment had been made in spite of the king's disapproval and had cost Stratford a simoniacal £1,000 to the younger Despenser.[1] And it was the growing general

---

[1] K. Edwards, *English bishops during the reign of Edward II*, in *E.H.R.*, LIX (1944), 335 ff.

hatred of both the Despensers, as well as a dash of envy and jealousy, which also brought the queen and her friends the very significant support of Henry, the less belligerent brother and heir of the executed Thomas of Lancaster, and even the help of Edward's half-brothers Thomas of Brotherton, earl of Norfolk, and Edmund of Woodstock, earl of Kent.

The Despensers were much too shrewd not to have realized which way the winds were blowing, but their astonishing successes had bred in them a fatal over-confidence. In September 1324, they advised Edward to sequestrate Isabella's estates on the grounds that there was a danger of an invasion from France – and, after all, she was a Frenchwoman. True, Isabella was reasonably provided for – she was granted an allowance of 2,920 marks a year, which was more than she had received from the Bardi in 1318, and the queen mother Margaret had been similarly treated for similar reasons in 1317.[1] On the other hand, and it was this which must have embittered Isabella, she had to submit to the installation of the younger Despenser's wife as her 'housekeeper' – in fact, as a spy of the Despensers with the right to superintend every detail of her correspondence.[2] It is little wonder that the rumours of marital discord became louder, and one chronicler suggests that at this time the younger Despenser was actually attempting to obtain a papal annulment of the marriage.

A significant incident, late in 1323, had marked the beginning of the new opposition grouping. Bishop Orleton, with the help of two wealthy Londoners, John de Gisors and Richard de Bettoyne, had organized the escape of Roger Mortimer of Wigmore from the Tower of London. His guards had been drugged 'by means of a drinking feast cunningly contrived', and Mortimer had escaped by rope-ladder over the walls and then over the Thames to the south bank and the road to Porchester and France, where he had traitorously offered his help to the French king during the Saint Sardos episode.[3] All that Edward's

---

[1] *Rymer*, II, 569; Tout, *Place*, 140–1; *Lanercost*, 249.
[2] *Baker*, 18.
[3] *Chron. Lond.*, II, 28; E. L. G. Stones in *E.H.R.*, LXVI (1951), 97–8; *Trokelowe*, 146. His uncle Sir Roger Mortimer, lord of Chirk, did not escape, and died in the Tower – some said of starvation – in 1326.

fury could accomplish was to banish Mortimer as a traitor, and to deprive Bishop Orleton of his temporalities – the Church refused to agree to any more drastic penalties. This escape of one of Edward's bitterest enemies – Mortimer had been very lucky not to have been executed after Boroughbridge – the mishandling and misfortunes of the Saint Sardos affair, the acquisitiveness and tactlessness of both the Despensers, the widening breach between king and queen, and the folly of the Despensers in allowing Isabella to go to France now left Edward deserted by the majority of the magnates lay and clerical. Even his old friend the archbishop of Canterbury was estranged, owing to a childish quarrel with the very worthy Archbishop Melton of York over a matter of liturgical precedence. It was a sign of very bad political weather, and a very unenviable and lonely personal position, that at this time stories of miracles wrought at the Pontefract tomb of Thomas of Lancaster, and even at lesser rebels' tombs at Bristol, began to gain widespread credence. In St Paul's there had been a tablet erected by Lancaster to commemorate the Ordinances – and his other great deeds – which Edward naturally had had removed after Lancaster's execution. The Londoners remembered the pillar on which the tablet had been erected, and it now became a popular place of pilgrimage and the scene of reputed miracles. Moreover, Edward's fury at Mortimer's escape was foolishly vented on the London citizens, who, as a body, were blameless. The city's chosen officials were replaced by royal nominees, and Edward's temper cost him yet another valuable source of support.[1]

Why the Despensers ever agreed to Isabella's departure is a mystery – they appear to have underrated the queen's capacity for mischief and intrigue. It was to prove a fatal error.

It was not long before a group of dangerous malcontents were rallying round Isabella in Paris. Roger Mortimer of Wigmore was, of course, already there, and he was joined by the king's ambassadors to Paris – Stratford, bishop of Winchester, Airmyn, bishop of Norwich (who had been appointed bishop in spite of Edward's wish to promote his chancellor Robert

[1] *Chron. Lond.*, II, 26–7 and note.

Baldock); the earl of Richmond whom the Despensers had offended; Henry de Beaumont, the queen's French friend and brother to the lady Vescy, and the disgraced Edmund, earl of Kent, on his way back from his inglorious campaign in Gascony. Nevertheless, the queen faithfully carried out her diplomatic mission, and with some success. By midsummer 1325 her efforts had at least achieved an agreement with her brother by which Edward's occupied French territories were to be restored to him providing he rendered homage for them.[1] The only reservations were concerned with the Agenais and the castle of La Réole which were to be the subject of further negotiations. Edward's council agreed that he should go to Paris to do homage, but the Despensers were adamant that he should not take the risks involved. They feared the threat from the English exiles in Paris, and there was a new threat at home – Henry of Lancaster had been discovered in what appeared to be guilty correspondence with the disgraced Orleton, and in any event he had not endeared himself to Edward by recently assuming the arms of his dead brother and tactlessly raising a cross to his memory at Leicester.[2] And the Despensers could ill afford to allow Edward out of their sight – once royal protection was removed, too many enemies were ready to strike. The healthy Edward was persuaded to pretend that he was too ill to make the journey.

At this stage, the queen suggested to her brother that her son might be allowed to act for his father. Apparently, the papal nuncios had already mooted this suggestion, and there is no doubt that it exactly suited her secret plans. Charles IV agreed, and so did Edward and the Despensers. In September, Prince Edward, now thirteen years old, was created duke of Aquitaine and count of Ponthieu-Montreuil, and sent to Paris accompanied by Stapledon, bishop of Exeter. On 21 September he did homage on his father's behalf to his uncle at the castle of Bois de Vinçennes outside Paris.[3] Charles IV should immediately have restored Gascony and Ponthieu to Edward, but he still retained the Agenais as compensation for his losses. Edward, in

---

[1] *Rymer*, II, 601–2.
[2] *Vita*, 137.
[3] *Murimuth*, 44; *Vita*, 141–2.

anger at a piece of what he considered diplomatic chicanery, assumed the title of 'Governor and administrator of his first-born Edward, duke of Aquitaine, and of his estates', in order to get round the legal difficulty of asserting his own rights when his son had already surrendered them in Paris. Charles IV replied by once more sequestrating the duchy, and sending in his armed forces. But even more catastrophic events impended.

Isabella had found in Sir Roger Mortimer the lord of Wigmore a paramour to her liking, and a powerful ally in her conspiracy against the Despensers.[1] When Bishop Stapledon, who had escorted the young Edward to Paris, realized what was afoot, he hurriedly left France in disguise, and reported to the Despensers and the king that treason was brewing to boiling point across the Channel. A series of letters survive which Edward sent to his queen, to his son and to the king of France in attempts to persuade Isabella and her son to return home.[2] They are well and affectionately phrased, but very much to the point – and they were quite useless. By the end of 1325 Isabella's adulterous liaison with Mortimer was notorious, and the only reason she could find for not returning, and refusing to allow her son to return, was that she would be in danger of her life at the hands of the Despensers.[3] Her open liaison so shocked her brother that he refused to countenance her presence in France any longer, and the younger Despenser had urged him to the same course – even the pope was now against her. But Isabella was not easily dismayed. Posing as an injured wife, she and Mortimer left Paris and made for Hainault, where its count William II was won over to Isabella's side by the flattering promise of a marriage between his daughter Philippa and prince Edward, heir to the English throne. The betrothal had no authority from the English council, and certainly no approval from the English king, but it was authoritative enough to persuade the count (who was also count of Holland and Zeeland) to advance a part payment of Philippa's marriage portion, which enabled the now raging queen to raise a small

[1] *Baker*, 21.

[2] *Baker*, 20.

[3] *Baker*, 21; *Vita*, 144; J. O. Halliwell, *Letters of the Kings of England* (London, 1848), I, 25–37; and see below Appendix IV pp. 165–8.

army of Hainaulters under the command of the count's brother John, and to make active preparations for an immediate invasion of England under the command of Roger Mortimer of Wigmore.[1]

Meanwhile, Edward and the Despensers had realized the extreme gravity of the crisis. Ships were mustered, a system of warning beacons was planned, the Tower was prepared for action, special arrangements were made for keeping the capital under royal control, and the younger Despenser quietly prepared for the worst by withdrawing £2,000 in cash from his private bankers. But by now, although king and ministers might command, their subjects were no longer willing to obey. The chronicler of London writes that 'the English sailors did not wish to prevent the arrival of the queen and her son and their company by reason of the great hate they had towards Sir Hugh Despenser', and reports that many deserted and preferred piratical raids on the coasts of Normandy.[2]

On 23 September 1326, Queen Isabella, her son, her paramour, her English exiles and her hired mercenaries sailed from Dordrecht across an undefended sea to Suffolk. The 'she-wolf of France' was baring her fangs.[3]

[1] *Rymer*, II, 617–8, 623; *Baker*, 20–1; *Murimuth*, 46; *Vita*, 142–3.
[2] *Chron. Lond.*, II, 35.
[3] See below note 2, p. 144.

Chapter 13

CATASTROPHE

The queen's invasion made land on 24 September 1326 in the estuary of the Orwell near Harwich, and, after disembarking, the queen and her supporters spent the night at the earl of Norfolk's castle at Walton.[1] Letters were immediately dispatched to London asking for the co-operation of its citizens, but the London chronicler reports that, although ready to help, they were unable to answer 'for fear of the king',[2] who had hurried from the south coast to organize defence from his fortress at the Tower. Isabella herself was playing a cynical but shrewd role – she dressed in widow's weeds, and, as a claim on popular sympathy, first made pilgrimage to St Edmund's shrine at Bury. She then moved on to Cambridge where she stayed several days at the priory of Barnwell, and where her small force of under a thousand was soon reinforced with local gentry and such important allies as Edward's half-brother, the earl of Norfolk, Henry earl of Leicester, and a bevy of recalcitrant bishops.[3] From Cambridge the invasion forces moved on to Dunstable on Watling Street and only just over thirty miles from London. Edward and the Despensers – temporarily safe in the Tower – were issuing urgent but useless commands for mobilization and defence; they offered rewards for the head of Mortimer, and Archbishop Reynolds published a papal Bull against invaders (it had originally been intended for use against the Scots) at the cross in St Paul's churchyard. But, with the Londoners clearly demonstrating that they were on Isabella's side, the Tower was soon a poor refuge for the king and his

[1] *Ann. Paul.*, 313–14; *Rymer*, II, 643; *Baker*, 21; *Lanercost*, 25. In *Genesis*, I, 155, the landing place is said to have been 'on the Suffolk side of the river in the Hundred of Colness'. *Stubbs Chronicles*, II intro. xciii gives 'near Harwich at Colvasse'.
[2] *Chron. Lond.*, II, 36.
[3] *Knighton*, I, 432; *Murimuth*, 46.

14 Edward II – a carving in Winchelsea Church

15 Isabella – a carving in Winchelsea Church

rapidly dwindling entourage. Reynolds retired to his Kentish home to await events in safety, while Edward, both the Despensers, the earls of Arundel and of Surrey, and the chancellor Baldock decided to make for the west country, where Edward's popularity with the Welsh and the Despensers' local power might help to stem the swelling tide of revolution.

The Londoners were now in open defiance – they posted a second letter from the queen on the cross in Cheapside, and copies of it on their houses; it summoned all good citizens to side with the injured Isabella and rid the realm of the pernicious Despensers. They seized a reputed spy of the younger Despenser and beheaded him in the street. They next caught a more important royalist – Stapledon, bishop of Exeter and treasurer of England – as he was making for the sanctuary of St Paul's. They stripped him naked and executed him in Cheapside, together with his brother and two of his staff. The bodies were shamefully maltreated and buried 'without the offices of priest or cleric', and the bishop's head was sent as a trophy to Isabella, who thanked the London mayor 'for his late bloody act, which was styled an excellent piece of justice'.[1] The capital was now at the mercy of the mob – it forced the constable of the Tower to surrender and to hand over Edward's second son, John of Eltham, the children of Mortimer, Sir Maurice de Berkeley and Burghersh, bishop of Lincoln, and oaths were extracted from ecclesiastics and justices at London and Westminster binding them to Isabella's support. The tablet of Thomas of Lancaster commemorating the Ordinances was re-affixed to its pillar in St Paul's, and it was half-way through November before a semblance of civic order was restored. The London citizens who had helped Mortimer's escape from the Tower were rewarded immediately – de Bettoyne was made mayor, and de Gisors was made constable of the Tower.[2]

Meanwhile, the queen and her growing army of supporters had followed Edward's party to the west. With London safely theirs behind them, they marched through Wallingford to Oxford, where Edward's enemy Orleton, bishop of Hereford, preached treason from St Mary's pulpit. At Gloucester, the

---

[1] *Chron. Lond.*, II, 39; *Walsingham*, I, 181–2.
[2] *Chron. Lond.*, II, 38–41; *Ann. Paul.*, 315–17; *Baker*, 23–4.

head of Bishop Stapledon was Isabella's welcome if grisly greeting,[1] and there, too, many more of the baronage, including Percy and more Lords Marcher, joined her forces.

Of the king's and his few remaining supporters' next movements there are confusing accounts. But by 14 October, Edward had reached Tintern Abbey on the Wye, while the elder Despenser, earl of Winchester, had been dispatched to Bristol, where the royalists must have hoped for some support – it was a very vain hope. On 26 October, the city and castle of Bristol surrendered to Isabella without a blow, and, on the following day, the first official act of the rebellion took place – Winchester was condemned to a traitor's death before Mortimer and a group of magnates which included the king's half-brothers and Henry of Leicester. It was a travesty of justice, but, understandably, it followed exactly the form used (in which the elder Despenser himself had played a part) when Lancaster was condemned at Pontefract in 1322. The only difference was that Winchester, now sixty-four, was not excused any detail of the full horrors of the treason sentence – he was eviscerated and executed on Bristol's common gallows.[2]

Isabella and her supporters, of whom the leaders were Mortimer and Bishop Orleton, were already finding themselves in a legal predicament – the lawful king of England was missing. A temporary pseudo-legality for their actions was obtained by declaring that the young Prince Edward, duke of Aquitaine, was 'Keeper of the Realm' – an appointment by the baronage which could appear to be legal in view of the king's absence in Wales.[3] And at this stage there is no great certainty about the king's exact movements. Apparently, from Tintern he reached Chepstow, whence he sailed with the younger Despenser in an attempt to reach Lundy Island in the Bristol Channel. The island belonged to Despenser, and from there they might have planned escape to Ireland. But they were unlucky – contrary winds drove them back into Cardiff's harbour. They wandered about Despenser's Glamorgan hoping for refuge and

[1] *Murimuth*, 48; *Stubbs Chronicles*, II, 309. Stapledon's head had been sent to Gloucester by the Londoners.
[2] *Ann. Paul.*, 317–21; *Murimuth*, 49–50; *Baker*, 25–6.
[3] *Rymer*, II, 646.

help but finding none, and finally on 16 November 1326, Rhys ap Howel betrayed Edward to the pursuing Henry of Leicester at the abbey of Neath.[1] Chancellor Baldock and the younger Despenser were captured with the king. On the following day, Arundel was captured by John Charlton – he had escaped to Shropshire. At Hereford, at the end of the month, Isabella and Mortimer continued their lynch law. Arundel and the younger Despenser were hailed before some kind of tribunal under the presidency of Sir William Trussell, an old follower of Thomas of Lancaster. Both Arundel and Despenser forthwith were given the full treason sentence – Despenser on a gallows fifty feet high, with one of his adherents ten feet below him at his side. Baldock narrowly escaped the same fate, but as a cleric he was granted benefit of clergy and given into the care of Orleton, who imprisoned him in his London house. But the London citizenry refused to recognize the bishop's privilege and they seized the ex-chancellor and flung him into Newgate, where he soon succumbed to the rigours of his treatment.[2] The only royal supporter to escape immediate doom was the despicable Surrey – and the reasons for his good fortune will never be known; he was granted the queen's forgiveness and survived for another ten years.

Meanwhile, the problems of protocol and legal procedure were still worrying the new *de facto* government. On 20 November, the captive Edward of Caernarvon had to suffer a visit from one of the men he hated most – Orleton bishop of Hereford arrived at Monmouth to demand the great seal of England. It was duly surrendered and given into the keeping of the bishop of Norwich. It was, therefore, now possible to issue writs in the king's name for a full parliament, which was duly summoned to Westminster for December but later postponed until 7 January 1327. It was to be a momentous occasion.

Like Edward's post-Boroughbridge parliament at York in 1322, the Westminster Parliament of 1327 included representatives of the knights of the shires and the boroughs, together

---

[1] For Edward's wanderings in south Wales see John Griffiths, *Edward II in Glamorgan* (London, 1904), 192–231; *Murimuth*, 49; *Baker*, 25; *Ann. Paul.*, 319.

[2] *Bridlington*, 87–9; G. A. Holmes, *Judgment on the younger Despenser* in *E.H.R.*, LXIX (1955), 261–3; *Froissart, op. cit.* XIII; *Walsingham*, I, 185; *Ann. Paul.*, 320–22.

with representatives of the Cinque Ports and of the royal lands in south Wales. The Londoners, of course, had their own representatives, but, in addition, hundreds of the citizens crowded into Westminster Hall and overawed the parliament's proceedings. Whether it could ever be a legally constituted parliament in the absence of the king is arguable but irrelevant – it was as near to a national assembly as the fourteenth century could get. The king himself was now a prisoner in the care of Henry, earl of Leicester, who was treating him with all proper respect in his own great castle at Kenilworth.

No official records of the 1327 parliament have survived, but it was as unorthodox in its actions as in its constitution. Its purpose was made quite clear in the text for Orleton's parliamentary sermon of Tuesday 13 January 1327 – 'A foolish king shall ruin his people', and this was followed by an extraordinary three days of oath-taking at Guildhall in London, when representatives of every estate in the realm swore to support Isabella and her elder son to the death, and to keep whatever ordinances the parliament might promote. On the Wednesday, a sermon by Stratford, bishop of Winchester, was based on the significant text 'My head is sick'. On the Thursday, a third sermon, this time by the renegade Archbishop Reynolds, who had at last decided where his best interests lay, was based on the text '*vox populi, vox dei*' – a text which in view of the open adultery of Isabella and Mortimer was almost a sacrilege. He went on to announce that Edward of Caernarvon was deposed, and was to be succeeded, with the unanimous approval of barons, clergy and people, by his first-born son Edward. There is some evidence that six Articles of Deposition were read out to this assembly. They charged the king with incompetence, preference for unseemly advisers, the loss of Scotland and other territories in Ireland and Gascony, destruction of the Church and of many of his noble peers, breaches of his coronation oath, cruelty and general 'lack of character'.[1]

[1] *Brut*, I, 241; *Rymer*, II, 650; *Ann. Paul.*, 321; B. Wilkinson in *E.H.R.*, LIV (1939), 223–25; M. V. Clarke, *op. cit.* 178 ff. For the Articles of Deposition see Appendix V below pp. 169–70. W. Stubbs in his *Constl. Hist. of England*, *op. cit.* II, 379–80, followed by M. McKisack, *The Fourteenth Century*. *op. cit.* 90, mistranslates the reference to Gascony and Ireland.

The rebelling bishops had already attempted to persuade Edward to attend the proceedings. The bishops of Lincoln and Winchester had headed a deputation to the king at Kenilworth, and they had returned rudely rebuffed – 'he utterly refused to comply, nay, he cursed them contemptuously declaring that he would not come among his enemies or rather, his traitors'.[1] On 16 January a second deputation was sent to Kenilworth – it was much larger, and shows how desperately the rebels wished for a royal abdication to lend legality to their revolution. Two earls, Leicester and Surrey, three bishops, four barons, two abbots, four friars, two barons of the Cinque Ports, four knights. three Londoners and representatives of some lesser towns made up the formidable deputation, whose spokesman was the Sir William Trussell who had pronounced sentence on the younger Despenser. He urged Edward to renounce the crown, and he was supported by the bishops. Edward would be maintained in all appropriate state, and his elder son would take his place. But it was left for Bishop Orleton to add the sinister hint of blackmail – if the king were to refuse, the people might repudiate not only him but his children. Edward was a Plantagenet – he had cursed the previous delegation in fury, now, in the extremity of disaster and faced with the cruellest of threats to his family, he broke down in abject defeat. Half-swooning, and theatrically clad in a black gown of mourning, he faced the full delegation, and tearfully announced his agreement to their terms. Sir William Trussell renounced all homage and allegiance 'on behalf of the whole realm', and the steward symbolically broke his staff of office to show that the royal household was dissolved.[2]

Edward of Caernarvon's almost total isolation at this point was tragic. Only four of the clergy – Archbishop Melton of York and the bishops of London, Carlisle and Rochester – had the loyalty and courage to speak for him, but their voices were quickly muted. Even Archbishop Reynolds deserted to the

---

[1] *Lanercost*, 254.

[2] *Baker*, 26–8 following Sir Thomas de la More who was present; *Brut*, I, 241–2; *Lanercost*, 255–6; *Rymer*. II, 683; M. V. Clarke, *op. cit.* 186 ff.; *Ann. Paul.*, 324; *Walsingham*, I, 187.

enemy.[1] The king's half-brothers, the earls of Norfolk and Kent, had hated the Despensers more than they loved their Edward. Robert Baldock, the chancellor, and Robert Holden, the controller of the wardrobe, were the only great officials to stand by him. And his queen and her paramour were not slow to encourage the propaganda that the queen was the injured party, that Edward of Caernarvon was a craven homosexual, a mental deficient and probably a changeling. The only part of Edward's dominion where men were still prepared to fight for him was in south Wales,[2] and even there the greed, and arrogance of the younger Despenser had sadly injured Edward's considerable popularity.

On 24 January 1327, the accession of the fourteen-year-old duke of Aquitaine as King Edward III was proclaimed, and the new reign was deemed to begin from the following day.[3] A week later, Edward III was crowned by Archbishop Reynolds in Westminster Abbey, and a new parliament reversed the sentence on the executed Thomas earl of Lancaster, and so enabled the new figurehead of the state – Henry earl of Leicester – in future to call himself earl of Lancaster. The pathetic prisoner of Kenilworth had lost his throne, and behind the pleasant façade of the amiable Henry of Lancaster three loathed faces grinned their pleasure – the adulteress Isabella, her paramour Mortimer and the execrable Orleton.

A surviving deposed monarch is obviously an embarrassment to any succeeding regime, especially if he survives in his own country. Isabella and Mortimer were not altogether happy at the humane, and possibly lax, treatment which Edward was receiving from Henry of Lancaster, and Lancaster himself was now due to join the new king's first Scottish campaign – different and more stringent gaolers were urgently needed. The choice fell on Thomas, lord of Berkeley Castle near Bristol, and

[1] I cannot understand Professor McKisack's compliments to Reynolds in her *The Fourteenth Century*, *op. cit.* 93; but cf. K. Edwards in *E.H.R.*, LIX (1944), 340 and *Stubbs Chronicles*, II intro. xci, and his *Constl. Hist. of England*, *op. cit.* II, 385, where he remarks 'Reynolds, it is satisfactory to know, died of shame for the part he had played'.

[2] *Walsingham*, I, 83; *Higden*, VIII, 301.

[3] *Baker*, 26–8.

Sir John Maltravers. Berkeley had shared the captivity of his father Maurice after Boroughbridge. His father died in prison, and his castle and lands in Gloucestershire had been part of the younger Despenser's booty. Thomas Berkeley was, however, released shortly after Isabella landed, and married a daughter of Mortimer. He had no reason to treat the ex-king with leniency and he was now closely allied with the new powers behind the throne. Maltravers was married to Berkeley's sister, and, having luckily escaped from the rout of Boroughbridge, he had fled to France where he was soon a member of Isabella's following. He, too, had no reason to love the ex-king.[1]

Isabella and Mortimer, living in open adultery and clearly holding the reins of power, may well have been worried at this time by the rumours of plots for releasing Edward from his new cell in Berkeley Castle, and by a popular reaction in the ex-king's favour. One plot in fact temporarily succeeded. A Dominican friar named Thomas Dunhead, his brother Stephen and a band of conspirators from Warwickshire and the midlands, managed to raid and plunder Berkeley Castle and release Edward, and for a short time they sheltered him in Corfe Castle. But their success was shortlived – Edward was recaptured and sent back to Berkeley, Thomas Dunhead was horribly done to death and his brother disappeared.[2] A second attempt at rescue was being organized by Sir Rhys ap Griffith,[3] an avowed and bitter enemy of Mortimer, when the conspiracy was betrayed. Mortimer immediately sent instructions by an agent to one of his supporters, Sir Thomas Gurney, who was to go immediately to Berkeley and dispose of Isabella and Mortimer's embarrassment in any way he wished. Shortly afterwards it was officially announced that Edward of Caernarvon had died a natural death in Berkeley Castle on 21 September 1327.

The true story of the manner of Edward's death can never be known for certain. The Baker chronicle has the ingenious story

[1] For the closing scenes of Edward's life, T. F. Tout, *The Captivity and Death of Edward of Carnarvon* (Manchester, 1920), *passim* is indispensable.

[2] F. J. Tanquerey, *The Conspiracy of Thomas Dunheved*, in *E.H.R.*, XXXI (1916), 119–24; *Ann. Paul.*, 337; *Brut*, I, 249; T. F. Tout, *Captivity and Death, op. cit.* 17–24.

[3] cf. J. G. Edwards in *E.H.R.*, XXX (1915), 596–8.

that Bishop Orleton sent a cunning ambiguous letter in Latin to Edward's gaolers which could be translated 'Do not slay Edward: it is a good thing to be afraid', or alternatively, 'Do not fear to slay Edward: it is a good thing', depending on the punctuation.[1] Unfortunately for this fiction, Orleton was at Avignon at the time, and actually at odds with Mortimer and Isabella over his preferment to the see of Worcester. The story that Edward was slain horribly 'with a hoote broche putte thro the secret place posterialle', which showed no traces on the corpse, is in John Trevisa's translation of Higden's Latin *Polychronicon*, and, as Trevisa was vicar of Berkeley during Sir Thomas Berkeley's life-time, the story has a certain authenticity – it was repeated by Knighton, by the Brut chronicle, and the Westminster monk responsible for the chronicle of John of Reading. The Baker chronicle is further responsible for the story that Edward's gaolers tried to kill him by keeping him starved in a tiny cell made deadly by foul odours and other grievous hardships, but that his great natural strength was proof against their worst machinations. They therefore had no alternative but to smother him as he slept, and to complete their nefarious work with the help of the red-hot spit, and he asks his readers to believe that Edward's murderers were so inept, and the castle walls so thin, that townsfolk outside the castle were able to hear the king's dying shrieks. Amid so much lurid fiction, the only fact which seems well established is that Edward of Caernarvon was murdered, if not to the instructions of, at least with the connivance of Mortimer, and probably also of Isabella.[2]

The fate of the murderers is more certain than their methods. Mortimer's messenger of doom – Sir William Ogle – was later condemned but escaped and died abroad. Sir Thomas Gurney was later arrested by Edward III's commissioners in Naples, and died on his way back to England for trial and probable execution. The chronicler Murimuth, followed by the Baker

[1] *Stubbs Chronicles*, II, 317–18. The Latin text ran 'Edwardum occidere nolite timere bonum est,' cf. T. F. Tout, *Captivity and Death, op. cit.* 24–5; *Baker*, 28–34.

[2] *Higden*, VIII, 324–5; *Brut*, I, 252–3; *Ann. Paul.*, 336–7; *Baker*, 33–4; *Murimuth*, 52–5; *Knighton*, I, 446; *Lanercost*, 259; *Bridlington*, 97–8; *Walsingham*, I, 189.

chronicle, states that Gurney's corpse was in fact beheaded at sea. Sir John Maltravers later did such good service for Edward III in Flanders that after over twenty years he finally received a full pardon and died in honour in 1364. Berkeley was probably not guilty of the actual murder, but he was certainly responsible for the safe-keeping of any prisoner in his own castle. He was prosecuted early in the next reign, but, after nearly seven years, his plea of ignorance was accepted. He was declared guiltless and served Edward III faithfully and well in several French and Scottish campaigns and died in 1361. There was clearly a conspiracy of silence while Edward of Caernarvon was in prison, there was clearly an anxiety to cover up the details of his death, there was clearly no great enthusiasm for pursuing and prosecuting those who had failed in their responsibility for his safe-keeping. It is a safe inference that Isabella and Mortimer were determined that no exhaustive inquiries should imperil their own security. Meanwhile, the boy king was in a most embarrassing situation – he might have been willing to bring a Mortimer to justice, but could he be expected to arraign his own mother?

Edward of Caernarvon's funeral was delayed for over two months – the court had other business in Scotland – but on 20 December 1327, with hypocritically lavish honours and in the presence of Isabella and the new king, the corpse was interred in the abbey church of St Peter at Gloucester. The tomb immediately became a place of pilgrimage and a miracle-working shrine for the credulous. It was three more years before Edward of Caernarvon's son felt himself strong enough to call Mortimer to account on the scaffold, to banish his mother from state affairs, and to commemorate his murdered father with pious and worthy honour. Over the tomb, Edward III placed an effigy, which is an early masterpiece of English alabaster lying beneath a lofty canopy of fretted Purbeck marble and local oolitic limestone; and fortunately the whole composition still survives in splendour.[1] The financial proceeds from the many pilgrims who flocked to this majestic shrine enabled the monks of Gloucester to rebuild their abbey in the glorious 'perpendicular'

[1] *Archaeological Journal*, XVII (1860), 297–319 and 335–42; L. Stone, *Sculpture in Britain, The Middle Ages* (London, 1955), 160–2.

style which had become the new English fashion. In the honour
at last done to his father's memory, Edward III made up for his
tardiness by his magnificence. And there were still those who
believed that the Gloucester tomb did not contain the remains
of Edward of Caernarvon[1]. The rumours of his survival were
strong enough to convince the ex-king's foolish and unpopular
half-brother, Edmund of Woodstock earl of Kent, and three
years later Mortimer sent him to the scaffold. When Jean
Froissart visited Berkeley Castle in 1366 he made inquiries
about Edward of Caernarvon's end, and 'an ancient squire told
me that he died within a year of coming to Berkeley, for someone cut his life short. Thus died that king of England. Let us not
speak longer of him but turn to the queen and her son.' So
the conspiracy of silence never ceased, and Edward's queen,
after the execution of her paramour, was allowed to go into
comfortable retirement taking her secrets with her together
with an ample allowance of some £3,000 a year. She lived a
long life, mostly at her Castle Rising in Norfolk, and died in
1358; she was buried in the Franciscan church at Newgate in
London, and it is ironical that 'the she-wolf of France'[2] met
her peaceful end in the innocent habit of the Order of the Poor
Clares.

[1] *Stubbs Chronicles*, II intro. ciii–cviii; *Genesis*, I, 171–2; *E.H.R.*, XLIII
(1928), 203 ff.
[2] 'She-wolf of France, with unrelenting fangs That tears't the bowels of
thy mangled mate' T. Gray, *The Bard* (1757), II, i. Some chroniclers suggested that Mortimer was only one of Isabella's several lovers in Paris,
cf. *Baker*, 20–23.

EPILOGUE

No other English king has received such unanimous disapproval as Edward II. 'A big, dull unmannerly oaf'; 'a greater ninny never lived'; 'a weakling and a fool'; 'absolutely destitute of all those qualities which constitute Edward I's claim to greatness'; 'a scatter-brained wastrel'; 'totally unfit to rule'; 'a complete misfit'; 'the first king since the Conquest who was not a man of business'; 'a trifler'; 'an aimless man without poise or sense of values'; 'a brutal and brainless athlete' – these are some examples of the strong language with which distinguished historians have described Edward of Caernarvon's character and career.[1] Most of the chroniclers admired his physical assets – 'faire of body and grete of strengthe' – which reminded his contemporary biographer of the 'strength and comeliness of his father', but they too are unanimous in lamenting his idleness, his low tastes and his affection for unworthy favourites.[2] Is there anything to be said in Edward's favour?

The Articles of Deposition summarize the official criticisms of contemporaries.[3] They can serve as a useful text for an examination as to whether those criticisms were valid.

The first article maintains that Edward of Caernarvon was incompetent. It can be conceded that he had no great love for the routine of government, but his choice of ministers to be responsible for that routine was on the whole excellent. Gaveston was never a royal minister, but both the Despensers were, and both, whatever their faults, were models of efficiency and of exceptional ability. Stapledon and Baldock were brilliant administrators, and if Reynolds was a better actor than he was

[1] In order of mention, I quote from *Genesis*, I, 165; J. Mackinnon, *History of Edward III* (London, 1900); M. McKisack, *The Fourteenth Century, op. cit.* 95; T. F. Tout, *The Political History of England* (London, 1930), III, 236; K. H. Vickers, *England in the Later Middle Ages* (London, 1937), 84; H. Johnstone, *Edward of Carnarvon, op. cit.* 131; W. Stubbs, *The Constitutional History of England, op. cit.* II, 328; *Vita*, intro. ix.

[2] *Vita*, 37 and 40; *Higden*, VIII, 298; *Flores Hist.*, III, 173.

[3] See Appendix V below pp. 169–70.

an archbishop, his rival Melton of York was an excellent choice who, unlike Reynolds, remained a loyal friend and supporter of Edward to the death. If Edward loathed the all-powerful Thomas of Lancaster, his loathing was shared by most of his contemporaries and modern historians have disliked him almost as much – 'that most impossible of all medieval politicians' says one, 'vindictive, sulky and a traitor' says another.[1] Edward earned the support and friendship of two of the most disting-uished, the most honest and the most able of the rest of his baronage – Henry de Lacy, earl of Lincoln and Aymer de Valence, earl of Pembroke – and such lesser friends as John of Weston, John of Hanstede, and Gilbert of Clare were 'all men of good standing' and 'by no means the lowborn upstarts whom later jealousy represented'.[2] It is always difficult to judge a medieval personality from surviving correspondence because it will certainly be incomplete, and there is no means of knowing how much the scribes contributed. But there is nothing 'incompetent' about the very large number of Edward's letters which have survived, and in them is ample evidence to prove that he was a prince who never failed to go to extraordinary lengths to help his friends, and who never lacked a saving sense of humour. And in the only record which exists of his verbal dexterity in high diplomacy, he earned unqualified approval.[3]

But this first article of the Deposition couples the charge of incompetence with the statement that Edward preferred 'evil counsel to his own dishonour'. What is the truth about his relationships with Peter of Gaveston and the younger Despenser – because these are the counsellors to whom the author of the Articles is referring?[4]

[1] Tout, *Place*, 16; *Vita*, intro x.
[2] H. Johnstone, *Letters*, 70–3.
[3] See *supra* p. 103; E. Pole Stuart in *E.H.R.*, XLI (1926), 412–15.
[4] The mightiest kings have had their minions;
    Great Alexander loved Hephestion;
  The conquering Hercules for Hylas wept;
  And for Patroclus stern Achilles drooped.
  And not kings only, but the wisest men:
    The Roman Tully loved Octavius;
    Grave Socrates, wild Alcibiades.'
        Marlowe, *Edward the Second*, Act I, sc. IV, 391–7.
  The reference to Cicero is of course unjustified.

EPILOGUE

It is more than likely that Edward of Caernarvon was a homosexual, but that does not mean that he was *ipso facto* incompetent or stupid, or that he could not also lead a normal heterosexual life. As a homosexual he is in very distinguished historical company, as a heterosexual he was the father of one of our most spectacular kings and a remarkable family. The choice of Gaveston as his youthful companion was in the first place not his – it was the choice of his respected father, and Gaveston came to be hated by a jealous baronage not for his viciousness but for his waspish wit at their expense, his tactless pride in flaunting his royal favours, and a skill at the manly art of jousting which they could not equal. Only one chronicle specifically refers to sodomy between Edward and Gaveston – the Cistercian monk of the abbey of Meaux in the East Riding of Yorkshire – and his knife is somewhat blunted in that he does not complain of sodomy, but of 'too much' sodomy.[1] Edward's contemporary biographer in referring to Gaveston quotes David and Jonathan and 'a love which is said to have surpassed the love of women', but he was anxious to point out that Gaveston's unpopularity was mainly due to the fact that he was both a foreigner and an upstart.[2] Victorian historians have for the most part politely glossed over the issue – the relationship was 'innocent though frivolous' wrote Hume,[3] and 'it was reserved for a later generation to discover an element of vice in what his contemporaries viewed with pitying indignation as a stupid but faithful infatuation' wrote the benign Bishop Stubbs.[4] Most of the chroniclers, too, hesitated to be frank – they referred to Gaveston 'loving the king's son inordinately', Edward 'so much loved him that he called him his brother', and 'by exalting overmuch a man that he had loved' he caused 'slander to the people and damage to the realm', and similar phrases which can mean much or little as the reader is inclined.[5]

[1] *Melsa*, II, 355, but written fifty years later.

[2] *Vita*, 30.

[3] D. Hume, *History of England*, II, 328.

[4] *Stubbs Chronicles*, II, 2 and his *Constitutional History of England, op. cit.* II, 328–34.

[5] *Brut*, I, 205; *Higden*, VIII, 293–300; *Knighton*, I, 407–8; *Vita*, 191–2; *Lanercost*, 184; *Scalacronica*, 136; *Flores Hist.*, III, 188, 227–8; *Ann. Paul.*, 255; and cp G. L. Haskins in *Speculum*, XIV (1939), 73–81.

Modern historians until recently have been equally hesitant. Professor Tout maintained surprisingly that 'it is impossible to take these vague charges seriously'.[1] Professor Vickers stated that 'Edward was more unbusinesslike than vicious'.[2] Dr Conway Davies suggested that the charges 'should be ignored' because 'they are unsubstantiated'.[3] Professor Hilda Johnstone in quoting a medical critic of 1910, politely wrote 'still less need we go so far as to find the explanation . . . in the assumption that he suffered from what "medical science recognizes under the general name of degeneracy" caused by "a diseased condition of the brain"'. Maddicott, on the other hand, has no doubt that 'a homosexual relationship did exist'.[4] There is, however, general agreement that Edward's relationship with the younger Despenser was of a very different kind. Edward liked the man, gave him a very free hand, and generously rewarded him. Despenser was no mere carpet knight – he was clearly an able administrator[5], and it was not his inefficiency but his inordinate greed for landed possessions which brought about his own and his king's downfall. The truth would seem to be that, in the choice of his ministers, Edward of Caernarvon was far from incompetent, and if, in the choice of one intimate friend, there is strong evidence of homosexuality, there is no evidence that that homosexuality impaired his competence as head of state.

But the charge of giving way to evil counsel is immediately followed by the charge that Edward of Caernarvon was given to 'unseemly works and occupations' to the prejudice of the welfare of his realm. Edward's preference for the company of humble craftsmen, his patronage of 'theatricals', his passion for

[1] Tout, *Place*, 14.

[2] K. H. Vickers, *op. cit.* 136.

[3] J. Conway Davies, *op. cit.* 78.

[4] H. Johnstone, *Edward of Carnarvon, op. cit.* 131 and cf. Dr Chalfont Robinson, *Was King Edward II a degenerate?* in *American Jnl. of Insanity*, LXVI (1910), 445–64; Gervase Mathew, *The Court of Richard II* (London, 1968), 139; *Maddicott*, 83.

[5] B. Wilkinson in referring to the Despensers writes – 'the genius of these imaginative royalists illuminated the later reforming period and just possibly gives a touch of Disraelian conservatism to the reactionary Statute of York'. *Constitutional History of Medieval England*, (London, 1952), II, 10.

music, his love of such hobbies as woodwork and metal work, his skill at thatching, hedging and ditching disgusted contemporary monkish and baronial critics as much as they endear him to our twentieth century. Let it be admitted that for a normal medieval English king, Edward of Caernarvon's tastes were odd, outlandish and shocking, but, in pleading guilty to the second item in the Articles of his Deposition, Edward's shade can claim the approval of all who welcome a warm touch of common humanity in those who must walk the cold corridors of power.

The third item in the indictment maintained that Edward had lost Scotland and 'other territories and lordships in Gascony and Ireland, which his father had left him'. Edward of Caernarvon's reputation as a soldier can never recover from the disaster of Bannockburn, but the otherwise most sympathetic Professor Tout has rashly stated that Edward 'showed himself a coward on the battlefield'. The facts are, first, that Edward I had failed to win Scotland – in which case his son could not be said to have lost it: second, that Edward of Caernarvon fought eight campaigns against the Scots, four as prince when he earned the commendations of his father, and four as king when he never disgraced himself by any known acts of cowardice, and at Bannockburn he was reputed to have fought 'like a lion'.[1] Campaigning against the Scots in Scotland was no trivial task – the nature of the terrain and the nature of the opposition meant constant hardship and never easy victory. Neither 'the Hammer of the Scots' nor his son, nor his grandson was able to conquer Robert Bruce, but that does not prove that the son was any more of a coward or less of a general than his distinguished father. As for Gascony and Ireland, it is true that the little war of Saint Sardos was an inglorious affair, but Edward of Caernarvon was not in command. And if he must take the blame for the incompetence of his half-brother, he must also be given the credit for the successes of his generals who drove the Scots from Ireland, killed Bruce's brother, and reimposed English overlordship. Edward II may not have been a great general, but he certainly took his fair share of soldiering.

[1] Tout, *Place*, 236–7; *Trokelowe*, 86.

The fourth item of the Articles charged Edward with destroying holy Church, and also with putting to a shameful death 'many great and noble men of the land'. The founder of a great Dominican priory next to his favourite manor at Langley, the benefactor of St Albans, the faithful pilgrim to Canterbury and Walsingham, the prince who won popularity with the monks of Bury – how could this Edward be a destroyer of the Church?[1] It is, of course, true that his vengeance after Boroughbridge was unbridled, but his treatment of the despicable Lancaster and his supporters had certainly no taint of the unchivalrous treachery which resulted in the execution of Gaveston. It was a ruthless age, and those who resorted to civil war to obtain what they wanted knew beforehand that defeat meant automatically a traitor's death. Edward's father had acquiesced in the mutilations which followed the death of Simon de Montfort at the battle of Evesham,[2] and he had sanctioned the horrors of the death of Wallace, but whereas Edward of Caernarvon at least granted Thomas of Lancaster a comparatively clean death by decapitation, the 'she-wolf of France' and her paramour ensured that both the Despensers suffered the full penalty of a traitor's death. The fourth charge against Edward of Caernarvon was ill-founded and can be dismissed.

The fifth charge related to Edward's coronation oath. He was bound by that specifically revised oath to do justice to all, and to ensure that 'the just laws and customs that the community of the realm shall determine' were defended, obeyed and strengthened. In what way had he broken this pledge? The baronial opposition under Edward II had only one objective – to ensure that monarchy by prerogative was rendered subservient to the baronage. The 'community of the realm' was one day to mean an approximation to democracy, with a limited monarchy as a figurehead to a parliamentary system; in Edward's time it was an excuse for a baronial oligarchy. Edward could have pleaded guilty to this charge in that he had resolutely, and very intelligently, fought every effort of his barons to overrule him. He had in fact finally succeeded, and it was only the 'superbia' of the Despensers – barons themselves – which brought final

[1] *Walsingham*, I, 138–9.
[2] *Rishanger*, intro., xxix–xxxiii.

16 Edward II and Edward III – York Choir Screen

17 Edward II – a detail from the Gloucester effigy

overthrow, not from the people but from his faithless wife and a disreputable group of disgruntled magnates. In his treatment of councils and parliaments Edward II had a better record than his father or his opponents, and his sense of his own prerogative was entirely orthodox.

The final item of the Articles quoted Edward's cruelty, his lack of character and an incorrigibility which had 'stripped the realm'. Edward could not claim that he was less cruel than most of his contemporaries. After the battle of Methven, in the year before he came to the throne, it was said that he had been guilty of excessive cruelty against the Scots,[1] but neither his father nor his fellow peers would find harshness to Scots a crime, and of any specific acts of cruelty there is no evidence whatsoever. As to an incorrigible lack of character which had ruined his kingdom, it must be remembered that, during his reign, the 'troubles' with his baronage rarely involved the populace, he could not be blamed for the havoc wrought by marauding Scots, and he was certainly not responsible for the European famine of the years 1315 to 1317. 'The commonalty,' wrote Sir Thomas Gray, 'under Edward were not oppressed', and he had personal experience of his subject. In our own day, the great work of Professor Tout proved that the state of England under Edward II 'was not altogether unprosperous',[2] and Edward of Caernarvon deserves much of the credit for the organization of the Staple system which is usually awarded to his son.[3]

But if all the official charges against Edward II cannot wholly be substantiated, the sad and incontrovertible fact remains that he was a failure. But in many ways he was a likeable failure. The devotion of some of his personal male friends was as remarkable as his own devotion to all his friends – worthy or unworthy. After Bannockburn, when the young

[1] *Rishanger*, 230; H. Johnstone, *Edward of Carnarvon*, *op. cit.* 114; Barbour, *Bruce*, 452–7.

[2] *Scalacronica*, 150–65 – 'Les comunes de sonn realme furont en soen temps riches et maintenus en rendes loys'; *Genesis*, I, 165 – 'the people were much better off than under the glorious rule of his father. There was far less taxation, no extortions . . . far less conscription, no foreign service, no winter campaigns in Scotland'; Tout, *Place*, 214–15.

[3] *Lanercost*, 229; G. W. S. Barrow, *Bruce*, *op. cit.* 330 note and 385.

Donald earl of Mar, a nephew of Robert Bruce, was offered repatriation, he refused it preferring to remain with Edward in whose court he had been brought up and to whom he had become deeply attached. Of women, he could claim his stepmother Queen Margaret, the countess of Pembroke, who founded Pembroke College, Cambridge, and all his sisters as consistently devoted to him. For his wife Isabella he eventually came to have a great loathing, but until Boroughbridge their relationship seems to have been normally affectionate, and there are pleasant letters to prove it. It was the younger Despenser's treatment of her which finally roused her savage temper, and,,however much she deserved that treatment, both Edward and the Despensers were made to pay in full. It was said at the trial of Bishop Orleton, seven years later, that 'in preaching at Wallingford he had said that the king carried a knife in his hose to kill Queen Isabella, and he had said that if he had no other weapon he could crush her with his teeth'. Orleton was not a good witness against Edward of Caernarvon, but the violence he suggested was not unlikely in a Plantagenet – a race whose fury was as sudden, as unrestrained and as brief as their tears.[1]

It has frequently been said that Edward was illiterate. A medieval king was not expected to be a scholar, but there is some evidence that Edward was not as uncultured as his enemies have maintained. Apart from the disputed witness of the poem attributed to him, there is factual evidence that he borrowed books from the library at Canterbury (and failed to return them),[2] that the universities of Oxford, Cambridge and Dublin owe tribute to his patronage, and that he was something of an architect as well as a mason, and something of a nautical designer as well as a shipwright.[3] England's cultural standing in

[1] J. O. Halliwell, *Letters of the Kings of England* (London, 1848), I, 23–37; A. W. Goodman, *Cartulary of Winchester Cathedral* (Winchester, 1927), No. 233, 105, reviewed by C. Clay in *Journal of Soc. of Antiquaries*, VIII (1928), 123.

[2] See H. Johnstone, *The Eccentricities of Edward II*, in *E.H.R.*, XLVIII (1933), 264–7 and M. R. James, *Ancient Libraries of Canterbury and Dover*, intro. xlv–xlvi and 148.

[3] P.R.O.E., 101/408/15.

the early 1300s was never the equal of Italy – there was no English Dante or Giotto – but in Edward's day there were certainly great builders, as the cathedrals of Exeter, Wells, Bristol, Ely, York, and Chichester can still demonstrate. Moreover, when Edward had to choose a tutor for his son he appointed that scholarly Richard de Bury, who later became bishop of Durham and the learned author of the celebrated *Philobiblon*. Edward of Caernarvon was never merely a boor, but there is some justification for the not unflattering description that he might have been 'a country squire of the best and most enlightened type',[1] and the suggestion that 'in our own day, he might like a namesake have declined to play a role for which he felt himself to be unfitted.'[2]

And in a story which has to be overfull of failures, jealousies and tragedies it is pleasant to conclude with two items in lighter mood. It is recorded of Edward of Caernarvon's sense of humour that Jack of St Albans, the royal painter, was given fifty shillings by the king's own hand for having danced on a table before the king 'and made him laugh beyond measure'. And perhaps the kindest reference to Edward of Caernarvon in all the medieval chronicles is in Walsingham. He writes that 'when Scotland would openly rebel against him and all England would rid herself of him, then the Welsh in a wonderful manner cherished and esteemed him, and, as far as they were able, stood by him grieving over his adversities both in life and in his death, and composing mournful songs about him in the language of their country, the memory of which lingers to the present time, and which neither the dread of punishment nor the passage of time has destroyed'.[3] The first English Prince of Wales found his only mourners in the land of his birth, and in those credulous penitents who made pilgrimage to the noble shrine which his son so tardily erected to his memory in the abbey which is now the cathedral of Gloucester.[4]

[1] J. Harvey, *The Plantagenets, op. cit.* 76; N. Denholm Young, *Richard de Bury 1287–1345*, in *T.R.H.S.* 4th ser. XX (1937), 139–40.

[2] H. Johnstone, *Edward of Carnarvon, op. cit.* 131.

[3] G. G. Coulton, *Medieval Panorama* (Cambridge, 1943), 560; *Walsingham*, I, 83.

[4] Viscount Falkland's verdict is as follows: But you may object. He fell by Infidelity and Treason, as have many others that went before and

followed him. 'Tis true; but yet withal observe, here was no second Pretendents, but those of his own, a Wife and a Son, which were the greatest Traitors: had he not indeed been a Traitor to himself, they could not all have wronged him. But my weary pen doth now desire a respite; wherefore leaving the perfection of this, to those better Abilities that are worthy to give it a more full expression; I rest until some more fortunate Subject invite a new Relation.

APPENDICES

APPENDIX I

'Sire, will you grant and keep and by your oath confirm to the people of England the laws and customs given to them by the previous just and god-fearing kings, your ancestors, and especially the laws, customs and liberties granted to the clergy and people by the glorious king, the sainted Edward, your predecessor?' '*I grant and promise them.*'

'Sire, will you in all your judgments, so far as in you lies, preserve to God and Holy Church, and to the people and clergy, entire peace and concord before God?' '*I will preserve them.*'

'Sire, will you, so far as in you lies, cause justice to be rendered rightly, impartially, and wisely, in compassion and in truth?' '*I will do so.*'

'Sire, do you grant to be held and observed the just laws and customs that the community of your realm shall determine, and will you, so far as in you lies, defend and strengthen them to the honour of God?' '*I grant and promise them.*'

> Trans. from C. Stephenson and F. G. Marcham, *Sources of English Constitutional History*, London, 1937, p. 192. The Latin original of the fourth clause has '*quos vulgus elegerit*' and the French version '*les quiels la communalte de vostre roiaume aura esleu*' – *Rymer* II, 33 and 36.

APPENDIX II

I   First it is ordained that Holy Church shall have all her liberties, as formerly, as she ought to have.

II   Further it is ordained that the king's peace shall firmly be kept throughout the realm so that every man may come and go and tarry according to the law and usage of the realm.

VI   Further it is ordained that the great charter shall be kept in all its points, in such manner that any obscure or doubtful point in the said charter may be explained by the said Ordainers and others whom they call to them for that purpose, when they see occasion and season during their time of office.

VII   Further, because the crown is so much abased and dismembered by various gifts, we ordain that all gifts given to the damage of the king and decrease of the crown since the commission made to us, of castles, towns, lands, and tenements, bailiwicks, wardships, marriages, escheats, and releases, whatsoever they be, in Gascony, Ireland, Wales and Scotland as well as in England, shall be repealed, and we repeal them altogether, and they are not to be given again to the same persons except by common consent in parliament. And if such manner of gifts or releases shall be given henceforth, contrary to the aforesaid form, without consent of his baronage, and that in parliament, until his debts are acquitted and his state becomingly relieved, they shall be held to be null, and the taker shall be punished in parliament by the award of the baronage.

VIII   Since it was formerly ordained that the customs of the realm should be received and kept by men of the country and not by aliens, and that the issues and profits of those same customs, together with all the other issues and profits coming from the realm, whatever they may be, should come in their entirety into the king's exchequer, and be received by the treasurer and chamberlains and delivered for the maintenance of the king's household, and otherwise to his profit, so that the king might live of his own without making prises other than ancient dues and rights: which provisions have not been kept: we now ordain that the said customs together with all the issues of the realm as aforesaid, shall be received and kept by men of the realm, and delivered to the exchequer in the above form.

IX Since the king ought not to undertake war against anyone, or leave his realm, without the common consent of his baronage, on account of the many perils which may come to him and his realm; we ordain that the king in future shall not leave his kingdom or undertake any war without the common consent of his baronage, and that in parliament. If he does otherwise, and summons his service for such an enterprise, the summons shall be null. And if it should chance that the king should undertake a war or leave the realm by the consent of the barons, and it should be necessary to appoint a guardian in his realm, he shall appoint one by the common consent of his baronage, and that in parliament.

XIII Since the king has been led astray and ill advised by evil counsellors, we ordain that all such evil counsellors shall be put away and wholly removed, so that neither they nor others like them may be placed near him, or retained in any office of the king; and that other suitable persons shall be put in their places: and the same arrangement shall be made concerning the servants and officials of the king's household who are unsuitable.

XIV Since many evils have come about through such counsellors and such ministers, we ordain that the king shall appoint his chancellor, the chief justices of both benches, the treasurer, chancellor and chief baron of the exchequer, the steward of his household, keeper of the wardrobe, controller and clerk to keep his privy seal, a chief keeper of the forests on this side Trent, and one on the other side, and also an escheator on this side Trent, and one beyond, and the chief clerk of the king in the common bench, by the counsel and consent of his baronage, and that in parliament. If it should by any chance be necessary to appoint one of these ministers before the meeting of parliament, then the king shall appoint him by the good council which he has near him, till parliament. Thus it shall be done henceforth concerning such ministers, when necessary.

XV   Also we ordain that the chief keepers of the ports and of castles on the sea coast shall be appointed and created in the above form, and that these keepers shall be of this country.

XVI   And since the lands of Gascony, Ireland, and Scotland are in peril of being lost for want of good ministers, we ordain that good and sufficient ministers shall be appointed to guard them, according to the form contained in the last clause but one.

XVII   Also we ordain that sheriffs shall be appointed henceforth by the chancellor, treasurer, and others of the council who are present, or if the chancellor is not present, by the treasurer and barons of the exchequer, and by the justices of the bench; and such shall be appointed as are suitable and sufficient, and have lands and tenements out of which they can answer to the king or the people for their doings. None others than such shall be appointed. They shall have a commission under the great seal.

XX   Since it is well known and has been found by the examination of prelates, earls, barons, knights, and other good people of the realm, that Peter of Gaveston has misled and ill-advised our lord the king, and enticed him to do evil in various deceitful ways . . . we ordain, by virtue of the commission our lord the king has granted us, that Peter of Gaveston, as an open enemy of the king and his people, shall be altogether exiled from England, Scotland, Ireland and Wales, and from all the dominion of our lord the king, both on this and on the other side of the sea; and that he shall avoid the realm of England and all the above lands, and all the dominion of our lord the king, between now and All Saints' day next.

APPENDIX II

XXVIII   Since the people feel themselves much aggrieved because men are emboldened to slay and rob, because the king through evil council gives them his peace too easily, contrary to law: we ordain that no felon or fugitive shall be covered or protected in future for any manner of felony by the king's charter of peace granted to him, or in any other way, except in cases where the king can give grace according to his oath, and this by process of law and the custom of the realm: and if any charter shall be granted henceforth to any man in any manner, it shall avail nothing and be considered null. No open evildoer against the crown and the peace of the land shall henceforth be aided or maintained.

XXXIX   Likewise we ordain that the chancellor, treasurer, chief justices of one bench and the other, chancellor of the exchequer, treasurer of the wardrobe, steward of the king's household, all the justices, sheriffs, escheators, constables, inquirers into any matter, all bailiffs and ministers of the king, shall be sworn at the time when they receive their bailiwicks and offices to observe and keep all the ordinances made by the prelates, earls, and barons chosen and assigned for that purpose, and each one of them, without in any point contravening them.

> Trans. from H. Johnstone, *A Hundred Years of History*, London, 1912, pp. 209–12. For the original see *Statutes of the Realm* (London, 1810–28) I, 157, and *Rot. Parl.* I, 281–6.

APPENDIX III

These Scottish men are right hardy and sore travailing in harness and in wars. For when they will enter into England, within a day and a night they will drive their whole host twenty-four leagues [over fifty miles] for they are all a-horseback, without it be the trandals and laggers of the host, who follow after afoot. The knights and squires are well horsed, and the common people and other on little hackneys and geldings; and they carry with them no carts nor chariots, for the diversities of the mountains that they must pass through in the country of Northumberland. They take with them no purveyance of bread nor wine, for their usage and soberness is such in time of war, that they will pass in the journey a great long time with flesh half sodden, without bread, and drink of the river water without wine, and they neither care for pots nor pans, for they seethe beasts in their own skins. They are ever sure to find plenty of beasts in the country that they will pass through: therefore they carry with them none other purveyance, but on their horse between the saddle and the panel they truss a broad plate of metal, and behind the saddle they will have a little sack full of oatmeal, to the intent that when they have eaten of the sodden flesh then they lay this plate on the fire and temper a little of the oatmeal; and when the plate is hot, they cast of the thin paste thereon, and so make a little cake in manner of a cracknell or biscuit, and that they eat to comfort withal their stomachs. Wherefore it is no great marvel though they make greater journeys than other people do. And in this manner were the Scots entered into the said country, and wasted and brent all about as they went, and took great number of beasts.

From Lord Berners' translation of *The Chronicles of Froissart*, Globe edition (London, 1913), XVII, pp. 17.

APPENDIX IV

The late Professor Hilda Johnstone's handsome edition of *The Letters* of Edward of Caernarvon when he was Prince of Wales in 1304–5, together with the letters edited by J. O. Halliwell in his two volumes *The Letters of the Kings of England*, dating from the end of Edward's reign, present a remarkable and on the whole a pleasing picture of Edward II at the beginning of his career and near its sad end. It is always the case, when considering royal correspondence, that the letters may owe much to official scribes or official prompting. But, while remaining on guard, the modern reader can receive some genuine impressions of Edward's personality from the letters quoted in my text and from the following:

To Walter Reynolds, his Treasurer:–

> ... we specially ask that if you have a good stallion in your stud you will hasten to send it to us at our stud at Ditchling (Sussex) as fast as you can – the season goes quickly – and my men will take good care of it and return it as soon as the season is over ... (*Johnstone*, p. 31).

To his sister Elizabeth, countess of Holland:

> ... my dear sister as we have a beautiful white greyhound, we beg you to send us the white bitch greyhound you have – for we very much want to have puppies from them ... (*Ibid*, p. 116).

To the Earl of Hereford:

> ... we thank you warmly for the greyhounds and the bow that you sent us ... (*Ibid*, p. 117).

To Agnes de Valence sister of Aymer de Valence:

> ... Well we see and you shew us well that you are and wish

to be our good mother. And we pray you ever to continue this good will towards us. And if you wish for anything that we can do, inform us of it with confidence, as a son who would gladly do and procure whatever could turn to your profit and honour ... (*Ibid*, p. 70).

To the Mayor and Sheriffs of London:

Since we are bound to aid and support our dear and well beloved Lady Mortimer of Richards Castle [a friend and protegée of Edward's mother the Queen Eleanor of Castile] because our very dear lady and mother caused her to be married in this country: and we have heard that this lady is imprisoned in the City of London through the indictment of evildoers, and that she is put to greater hardship than is fitting seeing that she has not been convicted ... we beg you that for love of us you cause order to be given that she be relieved of the unreasonable hardships put upon her and be treated in the most courteous manner that the law allows ... (*Ibid.*, p. 34).

To the Abbot of Shrewsbury:

... Because Richard our Rhymer wishes greatly to learn the minstrelsy of the 'crwth' and we have heard that you have a good 'croutheour' with you, we earnestly beg you to command your 'croutheour' to teach Richard his minstrelsy, and to find sustenance for the said Richard in your house while he is dwelling there during his acquirement of the said minstrelsy ... (*Ibid.*, p. 114).

To the Proctors of the Papal Court:

... we pray you especially to help Berdino de Friscobaldi to secure a letter from our dear Father in God the Pope to the prior and convent of the friars of St Augustine in the town of Florence that they may give back to him Bonacors, his son, whom they have clothed in their habit. He is a young boy of thirteen, so we understand, and when he is with his father and friends he will choose whether he would remain with them or return to the said religious order. For we understand that he is kept so strictly that his father and his friends cannot

164

speak to him, nor can he make his wishes known to them . . . (*Ibid.*, p. 74).

To Walter Reynolds, his treasurer:

. . . we bid you to cause to be paid to Adam the Poteler [a wine dealer] of Reading . . . the money which we owe him, as well you know, and what we have already bidden you to pay on other occasions: so that he may not have to return to us again for the said payment . . . (*Ibid.*, p. 86).

To Walter Reynolds, his treasurer:

. . . Since we learn that Queen Marie of France and M. Louis her son will soon be coming to England and that we shall have to meet them and keep them company while they are over here; and it is desirable therefore to be well-mounted in respect of palfreys, and well dressed in respect of robes and other matters against their coming: we bid you to cause to be bought for our use two fair palfreys suitable for our own riding and two saddles with reins out of the best we have in the care of Gilbert of Taunton, and the best and fairest cloth that you can find for sale in London for two or three robes for our use with the fur and loops appurtenant; and, when you have provided these things, cause them to come to us where-ever we may be as soon as you can . . . (*Ibid.*, p. 34).

To the Treasurer [1321]:

. . . we command that ye provide sixteen pieces of cloth for the apparelling of ourselves and our dear companion, also furs, against the next feast of Christmas, and thirteen pieces of cloth for corsets for our said companion and her damsels, with table linen and other things of which we stand in need against the said feast . . . (*Halliwell*, I, pp. 23–4).

To Queen Isabella, in France, December 1325:

Oftentimes have we sent to you, both before and after the homage, of our great desire to have you with us, and of our grief of heart at your long absence; and, as we understand that you do us great mischief by this, we will that you come to us with all speed, and without further excuses.

Before homage was performed, you made the advancement of that business an excuse; and now that we have sent by the Honourable Father the Bishop of Winchester our safe-conduct to you, you will not come, for the fear and doubt of Hugh le Despencer; whereat we cannot marvel too much, when we recall your flattering deportment towards each other in our presence, so amicable and sweet was your deportment, with special assurances and looks, and other tokens of the firmest friendship; and also, since then, your very especial letters to him of late date, which he has shown to us.

And, certes, lady, we know for truth, and so know you, that he has always procured from us all the honour he could for you, nor to you hath either evil or villany been done since you entered into our companionship; unless, peradventure, as you may yourself remember, once when we had cause to give you secretly some word of reproof for your pride, but without other harshness: and, doubtless, both God and the law of our holy church require you to honour us, and for nothing earthly to trespass against our commandments, or to forsake our company. And we are much displeased, now the homage has been made to our dearest brother, the King of France, and we have such fair prospect of amity, that you, whom we sent to make the peace, should be the cause (which God forfend!) of increasing the breach between us by things which are feigned and contrary to the truth. Wherefore, we charge you as urgently as we can that, ceasing from all pretences, delays, and false excuses, you come to us with all the haste you can. Our said bishop has reported to us that our brother, the King of France, told you in his presence, that, by the tenour of your safe-conduct, you would not be delayed, or molested, in coming to us as a wife should to her lord. And, as to your expenses, when it shall be that you will come to us as a wife should to her lord, we will provide that there shall be no deficiency in aught that is pertaining to you, and that you be not in any way dishonoured by us. Also, we require of you that our dear son Edward return to us with all possible speed, for we much desire to see him, and to speak with him. . . . (*Halliwell*, I, pp. 27–9).

APPENDIX IV

To his son, Prince Edward in France March 1326:

We have seen, by your letters lately written to us, that you well remember the charges we enjoined you on your departure from Dover, and that you have not transgressed our commands in any point that was in your power to avoid. But to us it appears that you have not humbly obeyed our commands as a good son ought his father, since you have not returned to us, to be under government, as we have enjoined you by our other letters, on our blessing, but have notoriously held companionship, and your mother, also, with Mortimer, your traitor and mortal enemy, who, in company with your mother and others, was publicly carried to Paris in your train, to the solemnity of the coronation, at Pentecost just past, in signal despite of us, and to the great dishonour both of us and you; for truly he is neither a meet companion for your mother nor for you, and we hold that much evil to the country will come of it.

Also, we understand that you, through counsel, which is contrary both to our interest and yours, have proceeded to make divers alterations, injunctions, and ordinances, without our advice, and contrary to our orders, in the Duchy of Guienne, which we have given you; but you ought to remember the conditions of the gift, and your reply when it was conferred upon you at Dover. These things are inconvenient, and must be most injurious. Therefore, we command and charge you, on the faith and love you ought to bear us, and on our blessing, that you show yourself our dear and well beloved son, as you have aforetime done; and ceasing from all excuses of your mother, or any like those that you have just written, you come to us here with all haste, that we may ordain for you and your states as honourably as you can desire. By right and reason, you ought to have no other governor than us, neither should you wish to have.

Also, fair son, we charge you by no means to marry till you return to us, nor without our advice and consent, nor for any cause either go to the Duchy, or elsewhere, against our will and command.

P.S. Edward, fair son, you are of tender age; take our

commandments tenderly to heart, and so rule your conduct with humility, as you would escape our reproach, our grief, and indignation, and advance your own interest and honour. Believe no counsel that is contrary to the will of your father, as the wise King Solomon instructs you. Understand, certainly, that if you now act contrary to our counsel, and continue in wilful disobedience, you will feel it all the days of your life, and all other sons will take example to be disobedient to their lords and fathers. (*Halliwell*, I, pp. 35–7).

APPENDIX V

It has been decided that prince Edward, the eldest son of the king, shall have the government of the realm and shall be crowned king, for the following reasons:

1. First, because the king is incompetent to govern in person. For throughout his reign he has been controlled and governed by others who have given him evil counsel, to his own dishonour and to the destruction of holy Church and of all his people, without his being willing to see or understand what is good or evil or to make amendment, or his being willing to do as was required by the great and wise men of his realm, or to allow amendment to be made.

2. Item, throughout his reign he has not been willing to listen to good counsel nor to adopt it nor to give himself to the good government of his realm, but he has always given himself up to unseemly works and occupations, neglecting to satisfy the needs of his realm.

3. Item, through the lack of good government he has lost the realm of Scotland and other territories and lordships in Gascony and Ireland which his father left him in peace, and he has lost the friendship of the king of France and of many other great men.

4. Item, by his pride and obstinacy and by evil counsel he has destroyed holy Church and imprisoned some of the persons of holy Church and brought distress upon others and also many great and noble men of his land he has put to a shameful death, imprisoned, exiled, and disinherited.

5. Item, wherein he was bound by his oath to do justice to all, he has not willed to do it, for his own profit and his greed and that of the evil counsellors who have been about him, nor has he

kept the other points of his oath which he made at his coronation, as he was bound to do.

6. Item, he has stripped his realm, and done all that he could to ruin his realm and his people, and what is worse, by his cruelty and lack of character he has shown himself incorrigible without hope of amendment, which things are so notorious that they cannot be denied.

> Trans. from G. B. Adams and H. M. Stephens, *Select Documents of English Constitutional History*, (London, 1919), 99. For the original French see S. B. Chrimes and A. L. Brown, *Select Documents of English Constitutional History, 1307–1485* (London, 1961), 37–8, *Rymer* II, 650, and Twysden, *Historiae Anglicanae Scriptores Decem*, 2765.)

INDEX

INDEX

INDEX